SIMON & SCHUSTER

# Two-Minute Crosswords

SERIES 5

## David King

A FIRESIDE BOOK

Published by Simon & Schuster Inc.

New York  London  Toronto  Sydney  Tokyo  Singapore

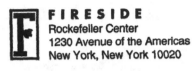

**FIRESIDE**
Rockefeller Center
1230 Avenue of the Americas
New York, New York 10020

FIRESIDE and colophon are registered trademarks
of Simon & Schuster Inc.

Designed by The Bedford Book Works Inc.

Manufactured in the United States of America

10 9 8 7 6 5 4 3 2 1

ISBN 0-684-81341-6
ISBN 13: 978-0-684-81341-7

# DEDICATION

For Gus, my sunny son

# ACKNOWLEDGMENT

Thanks to Joel Fishman for the idea,
the sale, and the contract.

# FOREWORD

Welcome to our fifth collection of miniature crosswords! This time out, we're going to bag spectacular specimens from around the world. Whether it's a clever clue from Kapandoto or a wonderful word from western Wotumba, we'll help you bring it back alive. As always, you'll find that these tiny crossword creatures are every bit as fascinating as the larger animals that also roam the land of puzzles.

At the start of your journey, you'll find the familiar species, well-known members of the crossword kingdom. As your trip continues, however, you'll meet more exotic creatures, some of which have never been seen in captivity. And as your safari nears its exciting end, you'll come face to face with the feral Final Five, beasts so brutal that few solvers will survive their encounters unscathed.

So, enjoy. But remember—it's a jungle in here!

Your comments and suggestions are important Please send them to:

David King
Author of *Two-Minute Crosswords*
Fireside Books
1230 Avenue of the Americas
New York, NY 10020

**SIMON & SCHUSTER**

# Two-Minute
# Crosswords

## P U Z Z L E  1

### ACROSS

1 Huge computer company
4 Chew in a grinding manner
8 Cat's cry
10 Hayworth of Hollywood
11 Olympic gymnast Korbut
12 Summit
13 Awkward and uncoordinated
15 Intoxicating element of beer or wine
18 Sandwich made on a long roll
20 *The Godfather* author Mario
23 __ horse (slang for "train")
24 One of Isaac's sons
25 Tear apart
26 Cried
27 Direction opposite NNW

### DOWN

1 __, *You're O.K.*
2 Abzug of politics
3 Bump encountered in downhill skiing
4 Sign of aging
5 Gentle bite
6 Chewed and swallowed
7 Coating put on a floor
9 "Be careful!"
14 Place to see lions and tigers and bears
16 Man-eating monsters
17 Detroit's football team
19 He wrote *The NeverEnding Story*
20 Bench in a church
21 "Oh, what's the __?"
22 Comic strip sound

## PUZZLE 2

### ACROSS

1 Confess
6 "A __ of Wine, a Loaf of Bread — and Thou"
9 Lying face-down
10 How many years old someone is
11 In the West, a steep hill standing alone
12 Opposite of healthy
13 Horrible
15 One sixtieth of a minute: abbr.
16 "__ hoppen?"
17 Skin markings made with a needle
19 Write quickly
20 Helpful
22 Anger
23 Varnish ingredient
24 What boys grow up to be
25 General direction of events

### DOWN

1 Important police broadcast: abbr.
2 Place to get prescriptions filled
3 Like sweaters that insects have gotten to
4 Whole and undamaged
5 Ball supports used by golfers
6 __ Rock (Elvis movie)
7 Really plain
8 Semiliquid/semisolid substance
14 Pair sold for the price of one
18 Injury, in a lawsuit
19 "Bad, Bad Leroy Brown" singer Croce
21 "Until the __ of time"

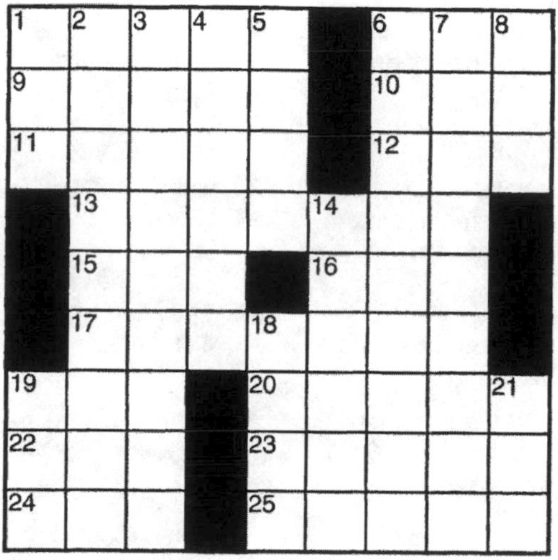

# PUZZLE 3

## ACROSS

1 One way a boxing match can end: abbr.
4 FBI agent, in slang
8 Advice columnist Landers
9 Capital of Egypt
10 Item used to protect your hand in the kitchen
12 Sigh of relief
13 Structure built by a beaver
14 Kick out
16 Children's book by Steig
18 Contribute to a crime
20 One of the vital signs
23 Islam's deity
24 Gibbon or orangutan, for example
25 Part of the hand
26 *The Hunt for __ October*

## DOWN

1 Strike a light blow
2 "Don't I __ you from somewhere?"
3 Alert and efficient, colloquially
4 Slang for woman or girl
5 Part of the organ of hearing
6 Vicinity
7 Character on *Cheers*
9 Way through a pasture
11 Prefix meaning six
15 Become weaker
16 Get rough from cold
17 Writer Walter __ Mare
19 What the winning runner of a race breaks
21 Animal like Aries
22 Actor Danson on *Cheers*

## PUZZLE 4

### ACROSS

1 By the __ of one's pants
5 Lively dance
8 Jeweler's measure for gold
10 "It's __-win situation"
11 Desert plant with stiff, sword-shaped leaves
12 Executive responsible for a corporation's funds: abbr.
13 __ off the old block
14 Young goat
15 Beatles album and film
17 Device for moving air around a room
18 Pitching great Hershiser
19 "I cannot tell a __"
20 "Time After Time" singer Lauper
22 Cost an __ and a leg
23 *The Mary Tyler Moore Show* actor Ed
24 It opens locks
25 Biblical city

### DOWN

1 The air above us
2 City in west central Wisconsin
3 Chief foe
4 Unspoken
5 Comedian famous for being cheap
6 First baseman, for one
7 "__ riddance!"
9 Starchy substance used to make puddings
16 Secret lovers' rendezvous
17 Criticism, slangily
21 Country whose capital is Dublin: abbr.

## ACROSS

1 Traditional month for weddings
5 Fellow, in England
9 Since
10 Cry of pain
11 Meat from cows
12 Man admired for his courage
13 Used as a home
15 California city: abbr.
17 Sentra or Acura, e.g.
18 Director Brian __ Palma

19 Seaman
22 Black double-reed instrument
23 Unsophisticated person
26 *The __ of the Cave Bear*
27 Pick through carefully
28 Clark __ (Superman's alter ego)
29 __ May Clampett

## DOWN

1 Poke
2 "__ only as directed"
3 "The First __" (Christmas carol)
4 Working without wasting effort
5 The quality of making sense
6 Having some shade of color
7 Sharp-smelling

8 "E.T. __ home"
14 Truck for moving furniture
15 Artist's shirt-like garment
16 Story by Aesop
20 Horse of a solid color
21 Actor __ Julia
24 Unwell
25 Take a plane

# P U Z Z L E  6

## ACROSS

1 Red felt cone-shaped hat
4 Repair
7 Leon who wrote *Exodus*
9 One on your side in a war
10 Money paid to a landlord
11 Short test
12 It's used to cool a drink
14 Vegetable in a pod
15 One name for God
19 Greenish gemstone
20 Revered person
22 Similar
23 Sticky material used to seal cartons
24 "Are we there __?" (Kid's car question)
25 Commercial cake preparation

## DOWN

1 Cat hair
2 "Able was I __ saw Elba" (palindrome)
3 Metallic element
4 Botch
5 Tennis player Nastase
6 Ending of the alphabet
8 "The Old Folks at Home" songwriter Foster
9 Scandinavian alcoholic liquor
13 Head of a corporation: abbr.
15 *Raging Bull* boxer LaMotta
16 Mark up a manuscript
17 Eve's partner
18 Arizona Indian tribe
19 TV talk-show host Leno
21 Luthor who fights Superman

# PUZZLE 7

## ACROSS

1 North Pole toy maker
4 Swift
9 One-man show about the writer Capote
10 Radiate
11 From A __ (the entire range)
12 Postpone
13 Open a clothing fastener
15 Person who roots for a sports team
16 Letters found at the end of a mathematical proof
18 And so forth: abbr.
21 Fast dance for couples
25 Grouchy guy
27 __ and yang
28 Army doll
29 Finish
30 Trail of a wild animal
31 "(Ghost) Riders in the __"

## DOWN

1 "__, Brute!" (Caesar's accusation)
2 __ Hubbard (founder of Scientology)
3 Slang word for police
4 Cayenne, for example
5 Tin Woodman's tool
6 "__ the Magic Dragon"
7 Light bulb, in a cartoon
8 Jurassic Park actress Laura
14 Score associated with mental power: abbr.
17 Accomplish
18 Dr. Seuss's Green __ and Ham
19 Excursion
20 Dog novel by Stephen King
22 Strong cleaning substances
23 Short, sharp bend in something
24 Humorist Rooney
26 Cow sound

## ACROSS

1 __ a plea (admit guilt to get a reduced sentence)
4 Apple pie __ mode
5 Some streets: abbr.
6 Weather problem after a drought
12 Animal used to pull sleds through snow
13 Kind of business that depends on catalogs
14 Abbreviation seen before an alias
15 Jellylike substance
16 In the twinkling of an __

## DOWN

1 Gristle
2 "On top of __ all covered with snow"
3 Musical composition suggesting rural scenes
6 Major political party: abbr.
7 It's north of Mexico: abbr.
8 Hit the slopes
9 Kind of strange
10 __ v. Wade (famous Supreme Court case)
11 Boss: abbr.

PUZZLE 9

## ACROSS
1 Mystery writer Lathen
5 Somewhat foggy
9 Wheedle
10 State east of Indiana
11 Tube used to convey water from a hydrant
12 "Honky __ Woman" (Rolling Stones song)
13 *The Hobbit* creature
14 Irish writer James
15 "__ Touch This" (M.C. Hammer hit)
17 Rule adopted by an organization
19 Center of activity
22 Animal's den
23 Number that means nothing
24 *The Diary of __ Frank*
25 Golden Fleece ship
26 Twist or swerve
27 Cheat in hide-and-seek

## DOWN
1 Repetition of a sound
2 Tie up a boat at a pier
3 Opposite of feminine
4 Cancel abruptly
5 In love with, slangily
6 Greeting to a sailor
7 Element used in galvanizing
8 Wooden frame used to harness oxen together
14 Bone that holds the teeth
16 Baseball's Rod Carew
17 Le Sage's *Gil* __
18 Jerk
20 Impulse to do something
21 "I can read him like a __"
23 Hit hard

# PUZZLE 10

## ACROSS

1 Fruity bread spread
4 Bearlike animal from China that eats bamboo
9 Chicken __ king
10 Book for a photo collection
11 President's wife
13 Religious creeds
14 Jacob's hairy brother
15 Abound
19 Dante translator John
21 Cold weather personified
24 Standoffish
25 "Zip-A-__-Doo-Dah"
26 Jazz bandleader Goodman
27 There are two in the word "llama"

## DOWN

1 Writer Rona
2 Name assumed by a criminal
3 Tony's love in *West Side Story*
4 Way through a forest
5 Outstanding sports performer
6 Boston Celtics' organization: abbr.
7 Bomb that fails to explode
8 Christian pop singer Grant
12 Madly in love with
16 Wear away
17 Famously unpopular car of old
18 Tiny bits
20 Questionable
21 Boxing punch
22 Pub drink
23 Opposite of pro

### ACROSS

1 Goes out like the tide
5 Exercise by running
8 Dr. Zhivago's love
9 Wolf, in Spanish
10 Spanish custard dessert
11 "Things are tough all __"
12 Allow to drift along
14 "Your time is __"
15 Be indisposed
16 *Alice __ Wonderland*
17 Certify by using a seal
20 "Sing us one of the songs of __": Psalm 137
21 Phnom __ (capital of Cambodia)
23 Movie and TV actress Swenson
24 "__ upon a time . . ."
25 School-related organization: abbr.
26 Robert Frost creation

### DOWN

1 One of the "Little People"
2 Kind of pen
3 Hillside in Scotland
4 Southwestern California city
5 Bon __ (rock group)
6 Kind of class for dogs
7 Bridge author Charles
9 Candy on a stick
13 *To __ with Love* (Poitier movie)
14 Open, as some garments
18 Garment worn at some frat parties
19 Ancient Greek philosopher
22 Garment border

# PUZZLE 12

## ACROSS
1 Cat with striped markings
6 Mixture of boiled fruit and sugar
9 Soap __ (type of daytime TV show)
10 Poet Lowell
11 Former president of Argentina Juan
12 Wood used for making archers' bows
13 Singer/songwriter __ Ono
15 Chemical symbol for sodium
16 James __ (11th president)
18 Polite, refined woman
20 "I __ not making this up"
21 Do the breast stroke, for example
23 Talk and talk
25 Broadway musical about the wife of 11-Across
28 First word of many book titles
29 Metric unit that's bigger than a quart
30 Large container
31 Kind of canoe

## DOWN
1 Blow one's __ (get angry)
2 *Tarzan, the __ Man*
3 Mineral whose varieties include emerald and aquamarine
4 Mel who directed *Blazing Saddles*
5 Sudden, strong pull
6 Blue bird that talks a blue streak
7 Correct the faults of
8 Sinatra's signature song
14 Pop singer Newton-John
16 Programming broadcast for extra fees
17 Biggest city in Nebraska
19 Friendship
22 Big-band leader who was a TV host
24 Animal around the house
26 Beverage made by soaking leaves
27 Noah's boat

**32**

33

# PUZZLE 13

## ACROSS

1 Jokingly tease
5 Coca-___
9 *Long Day's Journey ___ Night*
10 Peak
11 Gaiety and fun
13 Fiery place described by Dante
14 Peeve
16 Writer Rand who wrote *The Fountainhead*
17 Kid's mother
21 City in western Iowa
24 Apartment in an apartment complex
25 Sewing-machine inventor Elias
26 Water creatures that look like snakes
27 Grandson of Adam

## DOWN

1 Baseball Hall-of-Famer Palmer
2 $\frac{1}{2} + \frac{1}{2}$
3 Succeed when drilling a well
4 You honk it on a car
5 Arrived
6 What a surgeon performs
7 Controversial comedian ___ Bruce
8 Songwriter Hoyt
12 "___ I Had a Hammer"
14 Point being discussed
15 River in Germany
18 Courage, slangily
19 Creature known for being strong
20 Muscle soreness
22 $\frac{1}{2} + \frac{1}{2} + \frac{1}{2} + \frac{1}{2}$
23 Opposite of no

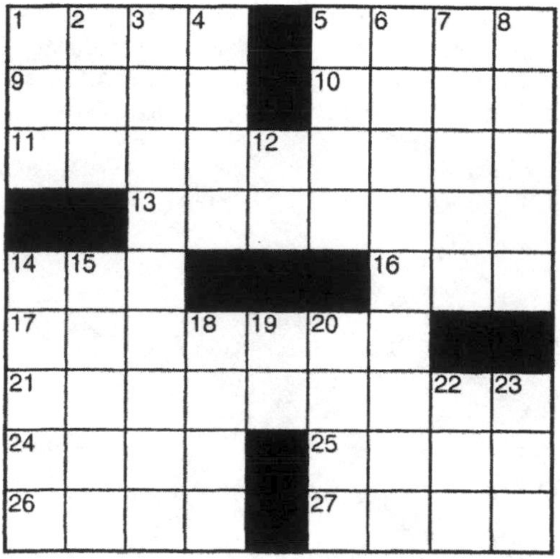
1 2 3 4 5 6 7 8
9 10
11 12
13
14 15 16
17 18 19 20
21 22 23
24 25
26 27

### ACROSS

1 Cigarette ingredient
8 Opposite of deep
9 See eye to eye about
10 *When Harry Met Sally* . . . director Reiner
11 Reasonably good
12 Scatters and drives away
16 "Don't be absurd!"
17 "__ believe in yesterday"
19 Place to soak in hot water
21 Along the way
22 Resolute

### DOWN

1 Kind of ruler
2 1977 George Burns film
3 Actress/singer Benton
4 Alcoholic beverage
5 She was the queen of the Nile
6 "You Send Me" singer Sam
7 Possess
13 Classic Alan Ladd role
14 Company known for its spreadsheet
15 *On the Beach* novelist Nevil
18 "Yeah, sure"
19 Furniture for sleeping
20 Bricklayer's need

## ACROSS

1 Wedge into a confined space
4 In the __ (nude)
8 Courtroom defender Dershowitz
10 Shaped like the office in the White House
11 Actor Richard of *Pretty Woman*
12 ". . . yet __ o'er the land of the free . . ."
13 Health resorts
15 Beast of burden
16 Humongous thing
18 "That's silly!"
19 Sea swallow
20 "The __ love belongs to another . . ."
22 Not inclined to work
25 Lyric poems
26 Dark greenish blue
27 One thing a fortuneteller reads
28 Opposite of bright

## DOWN

1 Drinking spree
2 Drink that has hops
3 Kind of wetlands
4 Pole that sticks out from the front of a ship
5 Type of rays blocked by sunscreen: abbr.
6 "Could you do me a __?"
7 Make a muscle
9 Hiring relatives for jobs
14 Go __ (act wild and crazy)
16 *A Fish Called* __
17 Stopped
18 Basketball player's goal
21 Fish that has no fins
23 Chinese leader Chou En-__
24 *A Nightmare on* __ *Street*

# PUZZLE 16

## ACROSS

1 Slang term for a gangland leader
6 Final letter
9 XXX movie
11 Mound of stuff
12 At a __ for words
13 Country in northeast South America
15 Gambling proposition
16 *The Fresh Prince of* __
19 "How __ Be Sure?"
20 Band of fir around an animal's neck
23 Horror movie sequel of 1986
25 Southern neighbor of Canada: abbr.
26 Wing added to a building

## DOWN

1 Speed-limit unit: abbr.
2 Fish eggs
3 Boast
4 Opposite of privately
5 Leave
6 The land of Israel, figuratively
7 *Born Free* lioness
8 Letters before ens
10 It's used to press clothes
14 Affirmative vote, old-style
16 Lowest voice in a choir
17 New Age music star
18 Destroy irreparably
19 Brains of a computer: abbr.
21 "Fee __ foe fum!"
22 Mend
24 Chuckle sound

## ACROSS

1 1966 Michael Caine movie
6 Sports car, slangily
9 Gets a baby to give up the bottle
10 "__ Gotta Be Me"
11 Late-night talk-show host Dave
13 Li'l Abner's Daisy __
14 Having the power
15 Organization that put a man on the moon: abbr.
16 Exactly
17 Half-open
18 Follower of Attila
19 Kids' jumping game
22 Geller who claims psychic powers
23 Hawaiian hello
24 Flavor-enhancing ingredient: abbr.
25 Poet Stephen Vincent __

## DOWN

1 Belt-maker's tool
2 He played the Six Million Dollar Man
3 Very obese
4 Crying
5 Compass direction opposite WNW
6 Former pitcher who wrote *Ball Four*
7 Danger for mountain climbers
8 French playwright Jean
12 Extremely messy apartment
15 Bible book about a prophet
20 Taxi
21 *The Cat in the* __

### ACROSS

1 Hits hard
7 Nonsense words sung in some songs
8 Most-used road in an area, colloquially
9 Words in a book
10 Small pitcher
11 White __ sheet (very pale)
12 Kind of poem written by Keats
13 Plane that goes faster than sound: abbr.
14 Network of crossing lines
15 Wind-powered watercraft
18 Self-conceit
19 Opposite of breadth

### DOWN

1 Legal document that forbids something
2 Character Solo in *Star Wars*
3 Like King Cole
4 Herb of the mint family
5 Expression of approval
6 Drooped
7 System of paying money to support the government
8 Item left on an answering machine
9 Decoration used on a loafer
14 "Gee whiz!"
16 Army officer with three stars: abbr.
17 Sunk one's teeth into

## PUZZLE 19

### ACROSS

1 Be in agreement
5 World War II vehicle
9 Declare true
10 Bullets and bombs, for example
11 Tame animals kept as companions
12 Short business note
13 "Beauty is in the __ of the beholder"
14 Actress Streep
15 Making a racket
17 Northernmost borough of New York City
19 Not many
22 *Cafe au* __ (coffee with milk)
23 Slang word for fast, misleading talk
24 Bible book after Ezekiel
25 *Et* __ (and others)
26 Cry hard
27 Band leader Lawrence

### DOWN

1 Wisecrack
2 *Designing Women* actress Judith
3 Person or thing feared or avoided
4 Stammering sounds
5 Fictional spy Bond
6 Tool used for smoothing one's nails
7 Award given for TV shows
8 Game played with a cue stick and balls
14 Combine
16 In an open cask of liquor, ready to be drawn
17 Played a piccolo
18 Flatten completely
20 Opposite of good
21 Having little power
23 Glass __ (boxing weakness)

# PUZZLE 20

## ACROSS
1 "__ with his head!"
4 Here, in French
7 Outside of a grape
9 "The __ Love" (Gershwin song)
11 Custard-filled round pastry
13 "__ Really Love to See You Tonight"
14 Telegraph pioneer
15 Clock, for example
18 Dressed to the __ (wearing very fancy clothing)
19 Entertainment device in most living rooms
20 New __ (French island east of Australia)
22 Small bills
23 Element that's a gas
24 Medical professionals: abbr.
25 Letters of the alphabet after ems

## DOWN
1 Bibliography abbreviation
2 Archduke whose assassination started WW I
3 Doctor's charge
4 Put in jail
5 Make happen
6 What bacteria can cause
8 Difficulty with walking
10 "__ I Fell" (Beatles' song)
12 Acted depressed
16 Long-distance runner
17 *Dynasty* star Linda
20 Person in charge of an Army unit: abbr.
21 Word used before a maiden name

# PUZZLE 21

## ACROSS

1 Pet-lover's organization: abbr.
5 Member of Monty Python
10 Big city in Quebec
11 "See __ I care!"
12 Lower edge of a roof
13 At an unspecified location

17 Fixed routine
18 It's used to display home videos
19 Famous courtesan and spy
22 Pertaining to the study of the body
23 Formal agreement

## DOWN

1 18-wheelers, for short
2 As a matter of convention
3 Big city in Ohio: abbr.
4 Caught in the __
6 "Let me say that again"
7 *Let's Make a* __
8 Melted rock from a volcano

9 __ guitar (rock music instrument)
14 Exclaim in ecstasy
15 Blues pioneer James
16 Force out
20 Make short jumps on one foot
21 Simon and Garfunkel's "I __ Rock"

# PUZZLE 22

## ACROSS

1 Summits
6 Chubby, rosy-faced child with wings
8 Actress Hedy
9 Alien spacecraft
10 Patch up
12 Edible nut of a hazel
15 ___ de Janeiro
16 "Caught you in the act!"
18 Having a full, shapely figure
20 Actress Francis who was on *What's My Line?*
21 Dart aside

## D A

1 Free-speech organization: abbr.
2 Separate the wheat from the ___
3 Short biographical piece
4 Noteworthy period of history
5 It's used to ride a wave
7 Soft, white, runny heese
11 Pornographic
13 Minnelli of movies
14 *Do the Right* ___
17 *A Death in the Family* author
19 Andy Capp's wife

## P U Z Z L E   2 3

### ACROSS

1 Moves with a dragging motion, as the feet
7 Be prominent
9 One's complete collection of clothes
10 "To __ is human"
11 Hit with an elbow
13 Much __ About Nothing (Shakespeare play)
14 Newspaper wire service: abbr.
15 Stuck in a __ (doing the same thing over and over)
16 Old-fashioned oath
17 Regular or typical
21 "Free Fallin'" rock singer
22 Military conference with an enemy

### DOWN

1 Popular song by Hoagy Carmichael
2 Redhead, slangily
3 And, in German
4 Initials of the president after Hoover
5 Egg __ young (Chinese-American dish)
6 Make a slave of
7 Use cusswords
8 Boston __ (1773 protest against the British)
12 Hen
18 Doctors' group: abbr.
19 Where Garrison Keillor got started: abbr.
20 Marina __ Rey

# PUZZLE 24

## ACROSS

1 Indian tribe of Oklahoma
8 Reason to see a dentist
10 Pacino of Hollywood
11 Comedian/actor Stiller
12 Number associated with smartness: abbr.
13 Note before "re"
14 Replacement for the LP
15 Letter after lambda
16 Where San Juan is: abbr.
17 Upper atmosphere
18 Spanish word for "yes"
19 __ *Mice and Men*
20 In the morning: abbr.
21 "__ one ear and out the other"
22 The, in French
23 Brand of jeans
25 Prefix meaning together
26 What the IRS collects after a person dies
29 Brand of pain remedy

## DOWN

1 Not inclined to fade or run, as cloth
2 "Westward __!"
3 Pony player's system: abbr.
4 Win in chess
5 *Driving Miss Daisy* actress Jessica
6 Kind of electrical power: abbr.
7 Full of fanciful ideas
8 "Baby" frog
9 Time when night and day are the same length
17 She plays Peg Bundy on *Married with Children*
24 "The __ is mightier than the sword"
27 Former baseball star Cobb
28 __ *Kill a Mockingbird*

# PUZZLE 25

## ACROSS

1 Gives in
8 Proportionately
9 Strength, as of a drug
10 You may clench it when you're mad
11 "M-I-C-K-__-O-U-S-E"
13 Rembrandt, for one
17 Marriage license requirement, usually
18 Cow's mammary organ
19 *Rocky* series actress Shire
20 Lower limb

## DOWN

1 Fill with horror or dismay
2 Force to leave a packed place
3 Collapsible bed
4 Preceding
5 Rather of *60 Minutes*
6 And others
7 Agree to
10 Position of employment
12 He played B. A. Baracus on *The A-Team*
14 Like medieval music
15 Make muddled
16 Children's writer William

## PUZZLE 26

### ACROSS

1 Italian fashion designer Giorgio
7 Wireless telegraph pioneer
9 Singer Sumac
10 Spring flower with broad, pointed leaves
13 Capital of Kenya
15 Central Polish city
17 Divisible by two
18 As a group
20 "The __ bird gets the worm"
21 Wag one's tongue
24 Graduating college class
26 Declare not guilty

### DOWN

1 One of Alcott's Little Women
2 Male sheep
3 Phrase used in a married couple's address
4 Opposite of DC: abbr.
5 Words of denial
6 Accustoms to something undesirable
8 Words on a Valentine's Day card
11 "How Can __ Sure?"
12 What a bowling ball knocks over
14 Flowering shrub
15 Golfer Trevino
16 __ roll (doing well)
19 In __ (meshing well)
22 Actress Meyers
23 California's clock zone: abbr.
25 Type of mental test: abbr.

## ACROSS

1 Earring location
5 Sidewalk vendor's frankfurter offering
9 It's found above a newspaper article
10 Country north of Greece: abbr.
11 Nancy Drew creator Carolyn
13 __ and vinegar (type of salad dressing)
14 Semiformal jacket, for short
15 1994 suspense movie set on a bus
18 Body part between the waist and the upper thigh
19 Chemical obtained from belladonna
21 Silly verse
22 Put in a mailbox

## DOWN

1 In the habit of
2 Opposite of young
3 Swindle
4 Adams or McClurg
5 Complete disorder
6 Place for a vertical-lift aircraft to land
7 Ratio of 4 to 12
8 Real
12 Force out
16 Units of work, in physics
17 Chief magistrate of old
20 Writing instrument

# PUZZLE 28

## ACROSS

1 Communist leader __ Tse-tung
4 Combine together
7 Small, poisonous snakes
9 Margaret Thatcher of England, for one
10 Processed spread trademark
12 Long pastries filled with cream
13 "Cara-__" (1965 song)
14 Submarine sandwich, to some
18 It's used to brew a beverage
20 Like
21 Nobleman below a prince
22 Stroke an animal gently
23 Dr. Ruth's specialty

## DOWN

1 Computer made by Apple, for short
2 Tennis star Arthur
3 Oil cartel: abbr.
4 Chemistry pioneer Karl
5 Part of the eye around the pupil
6 Letters after "W"
8 Get rid of by charging low prices
9 Piece of furniture for sleeping
11 Country in central Africa
14 Sit for an artist
15 "I wouldn't think __"
16 Penguin in *Bloom County*
17 Wooden frame fitted around the necks of oxen
18 Baseball player's headgear
19 __-Mex (spicy cuisine)

## ACROSS

1 Metal container used for cleaning clothes
8 *To Kill a Mockingbird* author
10 Latin phrase used by Shakespeare
11 __ instant (very quickly)
12 Tall, slender grass growing in marshes
13 *Octopussy* actress Adams
14 One who's going to graduate: abbr.
15 Move off
16 Send out, as rays
19 Affirm
21 Use a whip on
22 Opposite of more
23 Maine before the Civil War, e.g.
25 Place in a door people peek through

## DOWN

1 Design imprinted in paper
2 Johnson who was on *Laugh-In*
3 Point guard Webb
4 That guy
5 Add ornaments to, as a Christmas tree
6 Arm bone
7 Adventure book and movie about the French Foreign Legion
8 Female reflexive pronoun
9 Sign one's name on the back of
17 "That makes sense now"
18 __ *Drive by Night*
19 Voice below soprano
20 Calf meat
24 "Pipe down!"

# PUZZLE 30

## ACROSS

1 "__ Maria" (Catholic prayer)
4 Film company of Japan
8 __ up (confuse)
9 Boycott leader Chavez
10 Hockey rink surface
11 Peruvian beast of burden
12 *Potemkin* director Eisenstein
14 Mental age divided by chronological age: abbr.
15 Peculiar
17 Main office of someone in command: abbr.
18 Something that is unique
20 Cars
22 Sound of sheep
23 Childlike and unsophisticated
24 Biblical boat that carried animals
25 June 6, 1944
26 Dr. __ (rap artist)

## DOWN

1 Friends, in French
2 Police unit that deals with gambling, prostitution, etc.
3 Make an effort
4 Cat or lion, for example
5 Country Washington was the father of: abbr.
6 Actor who played Klinger on *M*A*S*H*
7 Middle Eastern country
9 Make pure
13 Very pleasing, in '60s slang
16 Rot
17 Round of applause
19 Counterfeit
21 Aunt, in Spanish

# PUZZLE 31

## ACROSS

1 Snake sound
4 Device that produces light
8 Batman foe
10 Predatoriness
11 Twist together
12 "__ Willie Winkie"
13 Initials of the 19th U.S president

16 Spring centerfold's title
20 Renounce
21 Family member
22 Study quickly for a test
23 Subject of genetics: abbr.

## DOWN

1 Toss about
2 Classic Western of 1953
3 Ninth month
4 Places
5 Out of the same mold
6 She gives out parking tickets
7 Stick one's nose into another's business

9 Talk abusively
14 Symphony conductor's rod
15 Wolflike animal
17 *To Live and Die __*
18 Joining line, in clothing
19 Army rank: abbr.
20 Shape of a rainbow

# PUZZLE 32

## ACROSS

1 He played Dr. Kildare in movies
6 Bucks or dough
8 Small document
10 1989 "Weird Al" Yankovic movie
11 Picture of one's bones
14 *Wizard of Id* character who drinks
15 In the past
16 Captain __ (Peter Pan's enemy)
18 "Nope"
19 Painter Pablo
22 Opposite of hawkish
23 Barbecue grill location, often

## DOWN

1 Surprise attack
2 Call used to get a stranger's attention
3 Landing place for Santa Claus
4 Deer with big antlers
5 *Rebel Without a Cause* actor Mineo
7 Bring bad luck to
9 Public __ (subways, buses, and so on)
12 Andre of the tennis courts
13 "__ and a bottle of rum"
17 "Would I __ you?"
20 Slang word for a policeman
21 Actress Gardner

# P U Z Z L E   3 3

## ACROSS

1 Element after copper
5 Salt-N-__ (female rap group)
9 "Hey, what's the big __?"
10 Peak point
11 Weakest chess piece
12 Head of the Catholic Church
13 Trojan War hero
15 Hard substance gotten from tusks
16 Great: prefix
17 Open a bit
19 Rise rapidly
23 Overly enthusiastic, in slang
24 Bantu language
25 Person Cain killed
26 Short piece in a newspaper

## DOWN

1 Kind of postal code
2 Lupino of the movies
3 __ Haven, Connecticut
4 Cape __ (launching place)
5 People who photograph celebrities
6 Powerful adhesive
7 Vitality
8 Woodchopper's tool
14 Trot
15 Likeness
17 __ Khan
18 Short, straight blow
20 No longer fashionable
21 Spanish shout
22 Keep __ (say nothing)

## ACROSS

1 Make get out
6 ___ retriever (dog breed)
9 Solo
10 Letter after sigma
11 Toothlike projection
13 Football position
14 Country with 50 states: abbr.
15 Dirty old piece of cloth
16 Alcoholic liquor exported by Jamaica
17 Land toward which the wind is blowing
21 Having turned-down corners, as a book
22 Winged resident of Heaven

## DOWN

1 Roger Clemens stat
2 *Batman Forever* actor Kilmer
3 Common vow
4 Magician
5 Very valuable item
6 At a future time
7 *M*A*S*H* star
8 Hit with a club
12 Gambled
18 Omelet requirement
19 Look at
20 Crazed computer in *2001*

## PUZZLE 35

### ACROSS

1 Mingle, as at a party
4 Streep of *Sophie's Choice*
6 One who warbles musically
8 Single show in a continuing series
9 "Gotcha!"
10 Nick Price's org.
11 Got a canine
13 Rescuers
14 Mends socks
15 Burlesque's Gypsy Rose __

### DOWN

1 Pertaining to the Middle Ages: Var.
2 Makes angry
3 Instrument played with mallets
4 Slang term used for a Beatle
5 Bookkeeping books
6 William Butler __ (Irish poet)
7 Registers
12 It gets pumped up

# PUZZLE 36

## ACROSS

1 Sacred song
6 Refresh one's skills
8 "May peace __ with you"
9 Government mileage-testing org.
10 Give one's approval for
12 Heckle
14 Full of life
16 One of the Baldwin brothers
17 General Motors product
18 "__ pin, pick it up, . . ."
19 Aid in wrongdoing
20 Jr.'s father
21 Sleep for a short while
23 "I refuse"
24 "Eureka!"
27 Emotionally detached

## DOWN

1 Spin-doctor's specialty: abbr.
2 Waterway near Egypt
3 Small, poisonous snake
4 Tibetan breed of small dog
5 Greek "M"
6 "Stay on your toes!"
7 Omen
8 Alloy of copper and zinc
11 Former capital of Japan
13 Zuider __
15 British tavern
22 From __ Z (covering everything)
25 "I don't believe it!"
26 In case

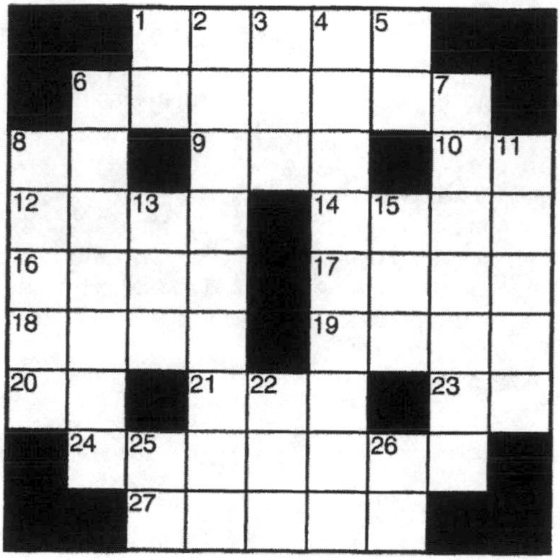

## PUZZLE 37

**ACROSS**

1 Quip
5 Trail left in the water by a moving boat
9 Morally wrong
10 China's continent
11 "__ the hall with boughs of holly"
12 Vehicles used by moving companies
13 Get on the nerves of
14 Tending to make sudden starts and stops

15 __ Boothe Luce
17 The "J" in "PB&J"
19 Put in stitches
22 Margarine
23 Think deeply
24 Kill
25 Big hunk, as of meat
26 "On the other __ . . ."
27 Tail end of a cigarette

**DOWN**

1 *Return of the __* (*Star Wars* sequel)
2 Vouch
3 Remove all of the flesh from the bones
4 Large North American deer
5 Go back and forth
6 Therefore
7 Put a bend in something
8 Not at all hard

14 *Bright Lights, Big City* author McInerney
16 Actor Bridges
17 Banter
18 Singer Fitzgerald
20 Name that means *hairy* in Hebrew
21 NBA point guard "Spud"
23 Authors submit them to publishers: abbr.

# PUZZLE 38

## ACROSS

1 Intern Perkins on *L.A. Law*
5 Son of Adam
9 Phoenix's rebirthplace
10 Provoke yawns
11 Get ready for something
12 Kind of camera lens
13 "__ the ramparts we watched . . ."
14 Seek out for comfort
15 Kind of test given by a psychologist: abbr.
16 Small barrel for beer
17 "Life __ the Fast Lane"
18 Used a microwave, slangily
20 1,400 in Roman numerals
21 'Twixt twelve and twenty
22 Two cards with the same number, in poker
23 Catch sight of, old-style
24 In addition
25 Soulful singer James
26 Schlemiel

## DOWN

1 Person selected for an office
2 In response to someone asking
3 __ Rabbit (Uncle Remus character)
4 "Uh huh"
5 Bella of politics
6 Welcome benefit
7 Sexually arousing quality
8 Suckable hard candy
14 Boston __ Sox
16 Nairobi is its capital
19 Took care of
20 Bamako is its capital
22 Rabbit's foot

## ACROSS

1 Popular, short-lived
   craze
4 Female spouse
8 *Alice* spinoff
9 Having a share of
10 Camera contents
12 Subsequent
13 Spelunker
15 Put into action

16 Female 6-Down
17 Sudden fancy
19 Unable to hear
22 Ballerina's garment
23 Underwater craft, for
   short
24 Pillow cover
25 Way to go over snow

## DOWN

1 Really, really loud, in
   music
2 __ Baba
3 *La* __ (Fellini movie)
4 Color close to
   cranberry
5 Inability to move
6 Small, wild canine
7 Show biz: abbr.

11 Greatest possible
14 Tick off
17 Lbs., ozs., etc.
18 Confused exclamation
20 Diving shorebird
21 Interstate law
   enforcement agency:
   abbr.

# PUZZLE 40

## ACROSS

1 "Swinging __ Star"
4 Amount of medicine to take at a time
8 Country south of Samoa
10 Actress Perlman who played Carla on *Cheers*
11 Custard-filled tart
12 1975 Spielberg whale movie
13 Austrian composer who wrote piano exercises

15 Similar
16 Part of a parachute
18 Tel __ (Israeli city)
19 Oblong portion of bread
23 Construction location
24 Plumb crazy
25 Former Russian ruler
26 Jinx

## DOWN

1 __-color (almost indecent)
2 Nothing
3 Steely Dan album
4 Mr. Hyde's alter ego
5 Main airport in Chicago
6 Stitched up
7 Opposite of difficult
9 Living the life of Riley

14 Nothing, slangily
15 Conservative activist Bryant
16 Plaster item for a broken bone
17 Hertz competitor
20 Exclaim in joy
21 The Red Baron, for one
22 *The Simpsons* network

# PUZZLE 41

## ACROSS

1 Sharp, temporary change of direction
4 Come to an understanding
8 Mouth shape
10 Vegetable pod used in soups
11 "Jabberwocky" creature
12 They're read by fortune tellers
14 Break into many small pieces
15 Hard water?

## DOWN

1 Game related to handball
2 Unusual
3 Carry in the uterus during pregnancy
4 High-ranking noblemen
5 Talk-show host Winfrey
6 In a higher place
7 *Lady Chatterley's* __
8 Bed that can be folded up
9 Basketball's Unseld
13 List ender

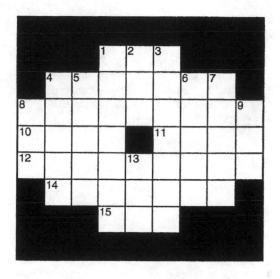

### ACROSS

1 First in importance
7 Gives a different designation to
9 Kind of baseball pitch
11 Native of Ankara
12 Extremely unusual
14 That, in Spanish
15 Evil spell
16 Place to buy things
18 Ridicule in a good-humored way
19 First name in the Renaissance
21 Author Theodore
22 Natural ability

### DOWN

1 For the time being
2 Rejection
3 Type of rays used for heating
4 Facial disguise
5 Unit of electrical current, for short
6 Lustful look
8 Ocean fish that swims in an upright position
10 German city known for china
13 Urge earnestly
17 Lawsuit word
18 Place for prisoners
20 Teachers' org.

## ACROSS

1 At that point in time
5 Land-measure unit
9 Item sought in medieval quests
11 One, in French
12 African tribal drum
13 Dad's partner
15 Org. that specifies what's officially an ounce
16 Top half of a bikini bathing suit
17 Craftsmanship
18 Turn brown in the sun
19 Average, in golf
20 Be neighbors with
24 Omaha's state code
25 Kind of sale
27 Seaweed
28 Start up a computer

## DOWN

1 Bulletin board fastener
2 Upstanding and honest
3 12th letter
4 Major Manhattan paper: abbr.
5 Upper limb
6 Light snooze
7 City in west Brazil
8 Where to find Freddy Krueger
10 Monopoly square
14 Former dictator Noriega
21 Faucet
22 "Live free __ die"
23 Seize suddenly
26 "Yes! We Have __ Bananas"

# PUZZLE 44

## ACROSS

1 George Bernard __
5 Hollywood's Randy or Dennis
7 Hawaiian volcano
10 Nevada neighbor
11 Athletic grp. for females
13 __ up (disgusted)
14 Gay dance
15 Piece of truth
17 Singer in U2
18 Chinese game which uses tiles
20 Shake awake
21 Cries of disgust

## DOWN

1 Patrol vehicle
2 "What in the world?"
3 Car owners' org.
4 Sly
6 *Wall Street Journal* owner
7 Make a mistake catching a baseball
8 Col. Hannibal Smith's old TV group
9 Doing well at, slangily
12 Eager
16 Old form of "you"
17 Nonsense
19 Container with a handle

## PUZZLE 45

### ACROSS

1 Johann Sebastian __
5 Steep rugged rock
9 Matty of baseball
10 Ms. Charlie Chaplin
11 One's concept of one's identity
13 Called fouls in a basketball game
14 Prefix meaning three
15 "__ wise guy, eh?" (Three Stooges line)
17 Confused
19 It attempts to match the stock market
22 Beer barrels
23 Words of understanding
24 Mates for rams
25 __ of the D'Urbervilles

### DOWN

1 __-relief
2 Give a warning to
3 The Rime of the Ancient Mariner poet
4 Tendency to be touchy
5 "Stop talking like that!"
6 Swayze movie of '89
7 Neighbor of Zaire and Zambia: abbr.
8 Glasgow "go"
12 Whether
16 Moorehead of Hollywood
18 Hatchet
19 President Eisenhower, for short
20 Recently arrived
21 Of the, in French

# PUZZLE 46

## ACROSS

1 Quick punch
4 They're used to support cameras
8 Soft drink brand
9 *Rebel Without a Cause* star
11 Stella D'__ cookies
12 Lacking moisture
13 Run after
17 Tell the story of
18 Completely finished
19 Wool provider

## DOWN

1 "__ Talkin" (Bee Gees hit)
2 *Planet of the* __
3 Fictional spy James
4 Russian empress
5 Taking off
6 Deadline
7 Less populated
9 Trot slowly
10 19th century humorist
14 Mystery writer __ Stanley Gardner
15 Cawing bird
16 Possess

## ACROSS

1 For humorous value only
8 Country whose capital is Minsk
9 Defensive wall
10 Greek god of love
11 Thin, rectangular piece of floor covering
14 Carpenter's tool
15 Commingle
16 Baseball great Musial
18 Poppycock
19 Lacking the ability for
21 One who delivers the mail
22 Distinguished

## DOWN

1 Head of a convent
2 French pointillist painter Georges
3 Weekly amount of money given to a child
4 Whale flick
5 ". . . man __ mouse?"
6 Writer __ Vonnegut, Jr.
7 Brand of frozen dessert
12 Lend an ear
13 Entreat
17 Language expert Chomsky
18 Go up in flames
20 Three: prefix

## PUZZLE 48

### ACROSS

1 Hole-punching tool
4 Letter before tee
7 Person between girlhood and womanhood
11 Therefore
12 Gumbo vegetable
13 Department store department
15 "Make less noise!"
16 Comedian Caesar
17 "For Once __ My Life"
18 Place one comes from
21 *The Good Earth* character
22 *King Kong* actress Fay
24 Notable character
26 Irritate mightily
27 Sunday seat, for some

### DOWN

1 Yes, in the Navy
2 Cavity found in old furniture
3 Racing sled used in the Olympics
4 For example: abbr.
5 Reduce one's speed
6 "For Pete's __!"
8 Balderdash
9 Type of ditch
10 Fiber used for knitting
14 Command to a dog
15 Buy stuff at a store
19 Sportscaster Albert
20 Shawl
23 Christmas tree
25 Strong as an __

# PUZZLE 49

## ACROSS

1 Perfect example
8 Ability to refuse to sign a bill
11 Pretentious, in a way
12 Former soccer superstar
13 Sticky and sweet
15 Month after Aug.
16 Logger's tool
17 Small bit, as of butter
19 Depart
20 Compete in an auction
22 Polyester trademark
24 Head of the Norse gods
26 Period before Easter
27 Sonority
29 Thick soup

## DOWN

1 *Green Acres* star
2 Hydrogen __ (bleaching agent)
3 *Leave __ Beaver*
4 Played cat-and-mouse (with)
5 __ art
6 Dusting tool
7 Rams' fans?
9 Refined grace
10 Newspaper employee
14 Sweet potato cousin
18 League rule
21 The "D" in "CD/ROM"
23 Do a credit union's job
25 Japanese dramatic form
28 Negative answer

# PUZZLE 50

## ACROSS

1 Billy the __
4 Old hat
9 Wedding words
10 Hawaiian greeting
11 Nancy Drew's boyfriend
12 Trigonometry functions
13 Work with minimum effort, colloquially
15 "The Grand __ Opry"
16 Stopped
18 Tennis shot
19 Raise in power or honor
21 Once more
23 Armani fragrance
24 __ over (ponders)
25 Extraterrestrial's ship
26 Pretty young woman
27 "__ Blu Dipinto Di Blu"

## DOWN

1 Sort or type
2 Zealous advocate of a particular doctrine
3 Game played in gym class
4 "Saw" for "see," e.g.
5 Actress MacGraw
6 "My gosh!"
7 How long a food can be stored without going bad
8 Make more bearable
14 Providing
17 Domesticated bull
18 Young sheep
20 Hammer or screwdriver, e.g.
22 Out of sorts

## ACROSS

1 Major TV network
4 "Born to Be __"
(Steppenwolf song)
8 Learning
11 The making of
decorative moldings
12 Strike suddenly
13 Soundlessly imitate
14 __ Aviv (Israeli city)
15 "Go away!", slangily
16 Military subgroup
18 Bridle part that's in a
horse's mouth
19 He stole from the rich
22 Couches, chairs,
bookcases, and so on
23 Person between
twelve and twenty
24 Word with a similar
meaning: abbr.

## DOWN

1 Former U.S. body that
monitored nuclear
tests
2 Act boldly, as if
without shame
3 Rum and cola drink
4 "You can't __ 'em all"
5 Bit of news
6 Given to carrying on
lawsuits
7 Building where college
students live
9 Short swim
10 No, in Russian
14 Gang's territory
17 Point on a fork
18 Food additive that
preserves freshness:
abbr.
20 Diary writer Anais
21 Cozy work room in a
home

# PUZZLE 52

## ACROSS

1 Assimilate
6 "__, Christian Soldiers"
8 Pain in the stomach
12 Separate sheet of printed material
13 "You look __ you've seen a ghost"
15 Golfer's warning cry
16 Former emperors of Japan
18 An act that serves as an example for a later one
21 Person who works with manuscripts
22 Run off to get married

## DOWN

1 What kernels grow on
2 *A Chorus Line* hit
3 Solemn
4 Indian term for a white person, in Westerns
5 "__ Little Tenderness" (Otis Redding hit)
7 Yellow flower
9 "They Long to Be (__ You)" (Carpenters hit)
10 "And I Love __" (Beatles hit)
11 Summer, in French
13 Rock guitarist's need
14 "To __ with Love" (Lulu hit)
17 "__ Dinah" (Frankie Avalon hit)
19 Letters after "M"
20 Three, in Italian

## ACROSS

1 British baby buggy
5 "The __ is up!" ("Things are hopeless now!")
8 Atmosphere
9 *Candid Camera* host Allen
10 Caresses an animal
11 Not __ many words
12 Use a credit card
14 Crankshaft-to-cooling fan connector
15 Awaken
16 Two cups
17 Makes good wine great
20 Suit to __
21 Singer/songwriter Lovett
22 Uncomfortable with attention
23 Actress Thompson

## DOWN

1 Mushed-up baby food
2 French word for street
3 He played Ed Norton on *The Honeymooners*
4 Love letter, in old slang
5 Kids' climbing structure
6 Picture in a picture
7 Ronny and the Daytonas hit
9 Event held to get rid of damaged goods
13 __ Dhabi
14 Unquestioning belief
16 __ de deux
18 Shade tree
19 Moon's __ of Tranquillity

## PUZZLE 54

### ACROSS

1 Makes a gesture
8 Region of Ethiopia
9 Scorn
10 Folk dance
11 Promised to work: abbr.
13 Hydrochloric __
15 Partly burn
16 Large inlet in the Philippines
18 Assumed
19 Orestes' sister
20 Ford Taurus model

### DOWN

1 Treat with drugs
2 First
3 "__ the season to be jolly . . ."
4 "__ be a pleasure!"
5 ". . . __ mouse?"
6 Person who lives near you
7 Southwest California city
10 Block a broadcast
12 Not wet
14 Protective dams
15 Main division of a long poem
17 Polish President Walesa

# PUZZLE 55

## ACROSS

1 Big butte
5 Blurt out
9 Funnyman Mort
10 Fully grown
11 Understand thoroughly, in slang
12 "By the Time __ to Phoenix"
13 Indian ruler
15 City of the Hawks
17 Shine unsteadily
18 Folk singer Baez
19 Shortly
21 Canadian pop singer Murray
22 Mexican Indian
23 Place to be under covers
24 Oversimplified ideas

## DOWN

1 Taste enhancer: abbr.
2 Hearing organ
3 System of speed writing
4 Type of battery
5 Guitarist for Queen
6 Become less serious
7 Make like
8 Wagered
14 Stick, as a zipper
15 Identically
16 Fragrance
18 Thrust
20 Short snooze

### ACROSS

1 Painting made on wet plaster
7 British conflict in South Africa (1899-1902)
8 Italian composer/violinist (1782-1840)
9 Where one takes a bath
10 Animal house
11 Character in *Miss Peach*
12 Meditative discipline
13 Wallet
17 Separate out from others
18 Quarreling

### DOWN

1 Thick, obscuring mist
2 "__ drop of golden sun"
3 Ending for "north" or "south"
4 __ stick (rod for stirring drinks)
5 Used a kayak
6 Constellation of a hunter
7 Ricky Ricardo's club on *I Love Lucy*
8 Strict adherent to tradition
9 Leg bone
14 Lawyer's degree: abbr.
15 Hula hoops, once
16 Extra basketball periods: abbr.

## ACROSS

1 E.g., e.g.
5 Stun suddenly
8 Customers
11 Item supposedly hidden by a bunny
12 Black Beauty, for example
13 Boxing match loser's famous cry
15 Former Boston Celtics coach Bill
17 Eager to get ahead
21 Detestable
22 In a __ (bewildered)
23 Fencing blade

## DOWN

1 Expert fighter pilot
2 Insipid
3 Animal on an old nickel
4 Modify a design to include later improvements
5 Zorro's mark
6 Math subject: abbr.
7 Al's wife on *Married With Children*
9 Michael of the Monkees
10 Formal, systematic article
14 Spoonful of ice cream
16 *Cocoon* actor Cronyn
17 '80s sitcom about a furry alien
18 Bossy's sound
19 Container for groceries
20 Behold

# PUZZLE 58

## ACROSS

1 Kind of tide
5 Weighing more
8 *Everything You Always __ Know About Sex . . .*
9 One who sailed to find the Golden Fleece
10 16 in Roman numerals
11 Place for a Pomeranian
13 Come before
17 TV newscaster Harry
18 Pours gently, as wine
19 Overwhelming victory

## DOWN

1 International defense organization: abbr.
2 Tied
3 Verdi opera
4 Peevish
5 Ivy League school near Boston
6 Train operator
7 Revolves
8 Variety of bean
12 For each
14 Mexican menu item
15 He sold his birthright
16 *They Shoot Horses, __ They?*

# PUZZLE 59

## ACROSS

1 In __ (compatible)
5 Corporation head: abbr.
8 Missouri River city
10 Vessel that landed at Ararat
11 Hall-of-Fame catcher
13 Group of vehicles traveling together
14 Burn slowly without bursting into flame
16 Darling, in French
17 Female servant of old
21 Charlottesville sch.
22 Broom-__ (cartoon witch)
23 *The Fresh Prince of __-Air*
24 Dolt

## DOWN

1 __ sauce (Japanese flavoring)
2 "M-I-C-K-E-__-U-S-E"
3 Continually carp
4 Root that's ground and mixed with coffee
5 Work with wood
6 Mistake
7 Give the nod to
9 Do away with
completely
12 Native to a region
14 Use a razor
15 Award worn on a uniform
16 What a golfer swings
18 Entirety
19 "What can __ for you?"
20 Mom's mate

# PUZZLE 60

## ACROSS

1 At no cost
7 Gain affection for
9 Evergreen shrub with flagrant flowers
10 Advanced degree: abbr.
11 Perceives visually
12 Basketball official, for short
13 __ *Sharkey* ('70s TV show)
14 *Exodus* author Leon
16 One, in German
17 Inhabitants
20 Trespass
21 Hypothesis that has some support

## DOWN

1 Yellow-and-black bird
2 Highway: abbr.
3 One __ time
4 Lots and lots
5 Unseemliness
6 Rising fairly sharply
7 Clear and consistent
8 Movie director Welles
10 Overly proper person
15 Title of respect used with a king
18 Menagerie
19 Play it by __ (improvise)

## PUZZLE 61

### ACROSS

1 Old man
4 Bone that Eve was created from
7 Bullring call
8 Freudian concept
9 It's found in chimneys
10 Cold-weather outer garment
12 Direction a compass points, almost
14 "__ On the Roof"
15 Growling sound
16 Exclamation of derision
17 "Almost Like Being in Love" musical
20 West __ Story
21 Baseball manager Ralph
22 Type of Buddhism
23 Parts of a pound: abbr.
24 Take in nourishment
25 Letter before kue

### DOWN

1 Item given to a lottery winner at a party
2 Felipe or Jesus of baseball
3 Cleaning substance
4 Dance party of the '50s
5 Composer Stravinsky
6 Building for storing watercraft
9 Returned parts of tickets
11 The "T" in "TGIF"
13 Gun-lobby grp.
18 Concept
19 Muck

# PUZZLE 62

## ACROSS

1 Wild hogs
6 Father, familiarly
9 Comic Bean
10 Cover a cake
11 Spaghetti or linguine, e.g.
12 Before, in palindromes
13 Sign of happiness
15 *Raisin __ the Sun*
16 Raise
17 Seasickness
21 Parseghian of Notre Dame
22 Stares open-mouthed
24 Japanese religious sect
25 Photographer Adams
26 Take a loss on
27 Make a god of

## DOWN

1 Short, sharp blow
2 Spoken
3 Attacker
4 Notably plump
5 Minor unexpected difficulty
6 Sugar-free cola brand
7 Unit used in measuring land
8 Moose, for example
14 Kind and decent
17 Minotaur's home
18 Kind of rug
19 "Zounds!"
20 Ship danger
23 Crafty

## PUZZLE 63

### ACROSS

1 Befuddled
6 Win __ nose
9 Wisconsin city
11 Past
12 Geometrically-patterned pictures
13 Not cooked as much
15 Replacements for vinyl: abbr.
16 Sharp, resounding blow
18 Dashboard stat.
20 Steak cut
23 Legal defense
25 Pea place
26 Fundamental reasons
28 Seer?
29 Pitching great Ryan

### DOWN

1 Remote
2 Ancient Roman garment
3 She lived with seven dwarfs
4 Ralph's pal on *The Honeymooners*
5 Extraordinary love
6 Dark semiprecious stone
7 Three feet
8 Luke's book, for short
10 Currently batting
14 "What was that?"
17 Type of truckers' radio
18 Female donkey
19 Drama
21 Hit for Tommy Dorsey
22 First garden
24 Sexually attracted to men and women
27 "Forget it"

## ACROSS

1 *2001* author's initials
4 One who walks a beat
7 Detective novelist Paretsky
9 "Parsley, __, Rosemary and Thyme"
10 Wove a web
11 Captain __ (pirate)
12 Medical __ (coroner)
14 Boob tube
15 Disparity between conditions
16 "I can't get __ satisfaction"
17 Overcome resistance with persistence
20 Bombeck of humor
21 Board used to make a table longer
23 Father of 4-Down
24 Leisure
25 Suspense writer Follett
26 AM radio dial label

## DOWN

1 Meathead
2 Country on a group of islands in the Atlantic
3 Essential point
4 Son of 23-Across
5 Light poet
6 Spanish version of "Peter"
8 Rearrange a word's letters to get a new word
9 Slalomer's need
13 "What me worry?" magazine
14 Twist and pinch
18 __ *For All Seasons*
19 Feeble
22 Moroccan city

# PUZZLE 65

## ACROSS

1 Pet-protection grp.
5 Baby carriage, in England
6 Shipping document
10 It's over the entrance to a theater
12 Pertaining to the environment: prefix
13 Tooth on a gear
14 "__ through the snow in a one-horse open sleigh"
16 Ocean route for ships
18 Scientology founder Hubbard
19 Border

## DOWN

1 Fashionable resort
2 Put on an undercoat before painting
3 Venezuela's capital
4 Writer Bierce
7 Mental-test number: abbr.
8 Red-haired comedienne Ball
9 Nimoy who played Spock
11 Holiday drink
15 "Ridiculous!"
17 Opposite of WSW

# PUZZLE 66

## ACROSS

1 Beginning of a branch
6 205 in Roman numerals
9 Japanese verse form
10 Cry of triumph
11 South American mountain range
12 Ink holder
13 Laugh half
14 Black Beauty, for example

16 All-around handyman
19 Wilson of cartooning
20 "__ Doo Ron Ron"
22 Cry of triumph
23 Buddy who played Jed Clampett
26 Michael Jackson hit
27 Philosopher Kierkegaard
28 "Make __ double"
29 Pinch

## DOWN

1 Ancient ruler
2 Straw head covering
3 Get __ of (toss out)
4 Eisenhower, familiarly
5 Quality of being effusive
6 Island in the Bay of Naples
7 Hardly shallow
8 It shows which way the wind blows

15 Yoke wearer
17 *The Mary Tyler Moore Show* spinoff
18 Note above "mi"
19 Mongolia's __ Desert
21 Henry VIII's II and IV
24 Bend at the waist
25 __ Lanka

## PUZZLE 67

**ACROSS**

1 Court and tort org.
4 Moisten meat while roasting
9 PC alternative
10 Revolutionary soldier Allen
11 Tree of the pine family
12 Tenderhearted
13 Fad item of the '70s that could be worn
16 Fork part
17 Fad item of the '40s that could be worn
20 __ contendere
21 Timber tree
22 Turns over
24 *The Crying Game*'s Stephen
25 Rope ring
26 Wetness that collects overnight

**DOWN**

1 Like some radios
2 Actor Scott of *Charles in Charge*
3 Site of the Parthenon
4 "Just __ yourself"
5 Chet of country music
6 Catcher's leg protector
7 Sharpness of taste
8 Termination
14 Sags
15 Decompose gradually
17 "*J'accuse*" writer
18 "Oh!"
19 Melt
20 Patriots' org.
23 "__ what?"

# P U Z Z L E   6 8

## ACROSS

1 Artists' area of Manhattan
5 "Love Me I'm A Liberal" songwriter Phil
9 Genghis __
10 It has a sole
11 Memo phrase
12 Critical point
13 Pea location
14 Broadway musical about the '60s
15 Rows, as of seats
17 Put a bad spell on
18 Metal used for cans
21 Mountain lion
22 Bogus talk
23 Adam and Eve's garden
24 Once again
25 Sit for shots
26 Pole that supports a sail

## DOWN

1 Hop, __ and jump
2 Words of worry
3 Dickens novel
4 "__ for the money, . . ."
5 Movie award
6 *Casper* star Ricci
7 Sixty minutes
8 Gender
14 Put a bad spell on
16 Empty and foolish
17 Art of gentleness, in Japanese
19 Engravers Currier and __
20 Politician Gingrich
21 Verve
22 Wedge

**144**

# PUZZLE 69

## ACROSS

1 Birthstone for October
5 Striker's org.?
8 Regaining of health
10 Small cooking pot with a handle
11 Month before Nov.
12 Final letters
13 Trim and tidy
15 Hindu sect member
18 Small marsh
20 Myrna of movies
21 Sudden, short spell of chilly weather
23 Veto
24 "You __ your britches!"
25 Light in the night

## DOWN

1 Actor Welles
2 "__ on earth, good will to men"
3 Superior in quality
4 Position: abbr.
5 Famous diary writer Samuel
6 Hard-shell, triangular, edible seed
7 Writer / philosopher Rand
9 Peeve
14 "Ready for renting"
16 Australian animal that looks like a bear
17 All nerves
19 Former Eur. country, now reunited
21 Corn on the __
22 Same-named fathers: abbr.

# PUZZLE 70

## ACROSS

1 Assign responsibility for an error to
6 Capital of Nova Scotia
8 Letter from Paul, in the Bible
9 Use a microwave oven, slangily
10 Peter, in Spain
12 Lazy
14 Loaded
15 It goeth before a fall
17 Oomph
18 Treats as identical
20 Sugar gotten from sugar cane
21 Smaller than small

## DOWN

1 "___-Blip" (Duke Ellington tune)
2 Speech impediment
3 Subsequent to
4 Island country southwest of Sri Lanka
5 Jog or do pushups, for example
6 Top part of an automobile seat
7 Decoration made by attaching one material to another
9 Oomph
11 Electrical resistance unit
13 Draw out
16 Officially merit
19 Jack-in-the-box, for one

## ACROSS

1 Former FBI director's initials
4 Grow gradually larger
7 Gardner of *The Barefoot Contessa*
8 Give a gun to
9 Iodine source
11 Buster Brown's dog
12 Render wiser
14 Make a subspecialty of
15 Barney Fife player
17 Rooney or Warhol
18 Lose one's cool
19 Pipe type
20 *Dos* preceder
21 Writer Rand
22 Gregory Hines film of '89

## DOWN

1 Copacetic
2 Tossup
3 Barney Miller player
4 Remain inactive during the course of something
5 Menem's country
6 Comic book group
10 Singer/comedian Lee
11 Beat fast
13 Geometric-figure suffix
15 Worf colleague
16 Food fit for pigs

# PUZZLE 72

## ACROSS

1 Small, steep waterfall
8 Turkish strait
9 Put away
10 Berkshire course
11 Iceberg victim
13 Get stopped up
14 Science show
17 Goddess of vengeance
19 Mr. __ (cartoon character)
21 Sort
22 Coccyx
24 '60s sitcom star Dick

## DOWN

1 Whitney's invention
2 __ it were
3 Full duration (of)
4 Trigonometry function
5 Trigonometry function
6 Performing pair
7 Superlative suffix
8 Remove water from
9 Common abbr.
12 Having been around for centuries
15 Just awful
16 Propose as a price
18 Melville's __-*Dick*
19 Kennedy's channel: abbr.
20 Assistance org.
23 Reasonable

# PUZZLE 73

## ACROSS

1 Give a wallop
6 Musical giant's initials
9 Actress Prentiss
10 Number of senators
11 Mystery's Hugo
12 Rev
13 Baseball Hall-of-Famer Delahanty
14 Frequent flier: abbr.
16 Idiot box
17 Finish
18 Neighborly letters
19 Model railroad scale
20 Hart's strip
21 Line of thought?: abbr.
22 Book cover word
23 Hollywood's Hagen
25 Place to get Seoul food
27 Common tattoo
28 Start of a Whitman line
29 Act the snoop
30 Semiconductor device

## DOWN

1 Parking lot feature
2 Horror movie cliche
3 Cal. page
4 Article
5 1984 Macchio / Morita movie
6 Sort of saw
7 It's 68 miles northwest of Fort Wayne
8 Farewell to a traveler
15 Dracula depictor
24 Irving of film
26 Crosby-Hope destination

# PUZZLE 74

## ACROSS

1 Chemical suffix
4 Neckwear
9 *Tonight Show* feature
11 Hard cheese
12 Introduced acts
13 *Notes on a Cowardly Lion* subject
14 Gear teeth
18 Dry, red wine
20 Persian religious teacher
23 Laos, Cambodia, and Viet Nam
24 Irritatingly bothersome
25 Mute an ad

## DOWN

1 Drive forward
2 Marilyn's real name
3 Tennyson's "__ Arden"
4 Liqueur flavoring
5 Spending green
6 Before now
7 Bank breaker
8 Service charge
10 Bake too long
15 Former president of Argentina
16 Davis of *Thelma and Louise*
17 Bra piece
19 Having a delicate open pattern
20 Go like the wind
21 Forming a whole
22 Some sts.

157

# PUZZLE 75

## ACROSS

1 Quibbling educators
8 Painting, sculpture, and so forth
10 Get for effort
11 Trim and tidy, shipwise
12 Hill dweller
13 G&S princess
14 Simpleton's sound
15 Care-giver: abbr.
16 Conglomerate
17 Arg. neighbor
18 High time?
20 Resembling
21 Drink made with carbonated water + lime juice
23 Hero hero

## DOWN

1 It's 100% fat
2 Umber, for one
3 Dull grayish-brown
4 Tool for the Tin Man
5 Pianist/singer/ bandleader Cole
6 Off-road vehicle
7 Gambling game
8 Kind of decorative work
9 Livingstone finder
19 Org. Bush quit
20 Display type: abbr.
22 Currently fashionable

# PUZZLE 76

## ACROSS

1 Sailor's "stop!"
6 Nuke
9 Act crabby?
10 Lummox
11 Ornamental design tool
13 Frat party staple
14 __ *Mutual Friend*
15 Orchestra leader __ Ray Hutton

16 Eye guy: abbr.
17 Rock's Morrison
18 Kipling book
19 Slip
22 Ring master of old
23 "(I Can't __) Satisfaction"
24 *Willard* sequel
25 *Beau* __

## DOWN

1 Lummox
2 Basinger, in *Batman*
3 Fight-or-flight hormone
4 "Just say 'no'," etc.
5 Util.
6 Comedienne in over 100 films

7 Rented room
8 *Treasure Island*'s blind beggar
12 Once-over
19 Adjective for the Beatles
20 Farm stand offering
21 "Tintinnabulation" user

## ACROSS

1 Potentially destructive thing
9 I strain?
10 Having no ties
11 K2, for one: abbr.
12 Woman's __
13 Scandinavian airline co.
14 Mom's twins?
17 Boffo show
20 Collector's item?
21 Oscilloscope display
23 Cursory cleaning
24 Madonna's ex

## DOWN

1 Contract conditions
2 "__ Name" (Jim Croce hit)
3 White lightning
4 CPR specialist
5 Quarter of a walk
6 "The __ Love" (R.E.M hit)
7 Act up
8 Low, in Lyon
15 Connoisseur
16 *Private Parts* author
18 Ancient Peruvian
19 Post-pubescent
21 . . . - - - . . .
22 Doo-__ ('50s music style)

# P U Z Z L E   7 8

## ACROSS

1 Cass Elliot and
   Michelle Phillips
6 Explore caves
8 USSR body of water
9 Novel about Dolores
   Haze
10 Hounded animal

11 GRF VP
12 Complete agreement
14 Applying a pre-paint
   coat
15 Tracks down
16 Ph.D. gauntlet

## DOWN

1 Supper, e.g.
2 Combined
3 Wild horses of the
   southwest plains
4 Lend __ (listen)
5 Jamaican music style

6 Macedonian seaport
7 Nearest
10 Commotion
13 Stops standing
14 Mideast radical group:
   abbr.

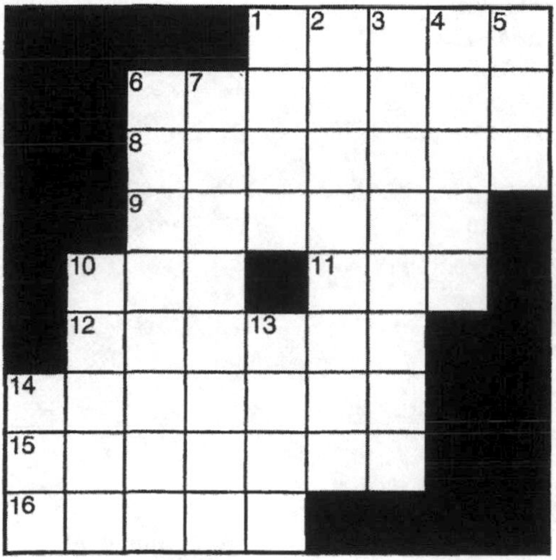
1 2 3 4 5
6 7
8
9
10 11
12 13
14
15
16

# PUZZLE 79

## ACROSS

1 Bertha Cool creator
7 1980 Nielsen/Curtis horror flick
11 Highlander
12 Nice god
13 @(@!! and *&^?#*
15 Puzzle
16 Chanukah top
18 Easy item?
19 Beats badly
21 To-do list entry
23 Each
24 Michelangelo of movies
26 Petrarchan form

## DOWN

1 Lhasa __
2 Pastoral
3 Ottoman
4 I __ Cheese
5 Amidst
6 Disencumber
8 Quit
9 Calcaneus
10 Semiformal wear
14 Grauman of Grauman's Chinese Theater
17 Exhaust gradually
18 "Harper Valley __"
20 Narrow reef
22 Finishes off
25 Word of denial

# PUZZLE 80

## ACROSS

1 Heaps of snow
7 Band leader Robertson
8 Pale yellow
9 Be in debt to
10 Sponsored messages
12 Put hair to string
13 Place for prayer
15 Boxing expert Fleischer
17 Stirrup site
18 Sticky situation?
21 ___ State (New York)
22 Talk aimlessly

## DOWN

1 Use as a source
2 Liquid that's a perfume
3 DEC competitor
4 CIA colleague
5 Brown at *The New Yorker*
6 Type of small, imperfect gem
8 Task
11 Harbor builder
14 Twisted
16 Writer Janowitz
19 Phonograph speed unit: abbr.
20 Chest protector

## ACROSS

1 Frequent Rock Hudson costar
9 What melanin helps determine
10 Strained
11 Run and Jam Master Jay's partner
13 T.S. Eliot's "The Rum __ Tugger"
14 "__ Blues" (Beatles' song)
15 Schoolmarmish
17 First of a famed film series
18 Long time
19 Come to comprehend
20 Good enough as is
21 Ready, willing and able
24 More restrained mood or atmosphere
26 Animal that often feeds on lemmings

## DOWN

1 Reason to move the hands: abbr.
2 "I'm broke, it's __"
3 Movie star found in a WWI trench
4 To put it briefly
5 Glass piece
6 Attend to
7 *Hill Street Blues* officer
8 Oman neighbor
12 __-Magnon
15 Zing
16 Emulates a buffalo?
17 Darling
19 Coal carrier
22 Morning moisture
23 Duvall role
25 __ *Exit*

# PUZZLE 82

## ACROSS

1 Unwholesome atmosphere
7 Really bad movie director
10 Caraway carrier
11 Tanner's need
12 "Texas tea"
13 Wastes
15 Tie
20 First president of the Fifth Republic
21 Sight stopper

## DOWN

1 Sea of France
2 Mt. ___ (Charlie Weaver's home town)
3 The fear of God
4 Film in which Julie Andrews bares her breasts
5 Leader of Prince's old backing band
6 *Let's Make* ___
8 Marijuana cigarette, slangily
9 Hwys.
12 Old enough
13 Unpaired
14 Chant start
16 Cry's partner
17 Extension type
18 Clay, today
19 One of the Kennedys

## ACROSS

1 Formally surrender
9 She's crowned with flowers
10 Brownish purple
11 Friend's address?
12 Start an inquisition
13 Short life
14 Penniless
18 Spun network
19 Fifth tone
20 "__ the Mood for Love"
22 Homicidally enraged
23 Defense type
25 Laced items, colloquially

## DOWN

1 Raise a smile
2 Stroke part
3 Color
4 Matthau movie
5 Perform satisfactorily
6 *A Shropshire Lad* poet
7 Price device
8 Vane dir.
10 Digs
13 Apron top
15 Campers' shelters
16 Roger and Jessica Rabbit, e.g.
17 Doe beau
20 Duplicate bridge scoring unit: abbr.
21 "__ Miss Your Apple Pie"
22 French friend
24 All right

## PUZZLE 84

### ACROSS
1 Bedlam
6 Become less active
9 March ender
10 "__ Marlene"
12 "Woof!" alternative
13 Actor Herbert
14 *Avril* successor
15 Monokini's lack

16 __ Saud (former Arabic ruler)
17 Vitamin stat.
18 Aerosmith metier
20 Racquetball target
21 Ultraformal
23 Lhasa location

### DOWN
1 She had "It"
2 Yard / 72
3 Play a part
4 Famed corral
5 The sun himself
6 Former Israeli prime minister

7 Remove impurities from
8 Like night baseball games
11 Transfix
19 Frontiersman Carson
20 World Wide __
22 Solfeggio syllable

## ACROSS

1 Disney film of 1942
6 Jail, slangily
9 Item used to carry papers
11 Undistinguished
12 Kiln, for one
13 Win over
15 Experiences
16 Endora's witch daughter
21 Freudian stage
22 Receive for service
24 Flirting
26 Penny prez
27 Suppress

## DOWN

1 Kid's shot
2 Not give __ (be uncaring)
3 Behave like Bip
4 Hitler's "__ putsch"
5 On condition that
6 Hirt hit
7 Practiced
8 Characteristic carrier
10 *Pretty Peaches* star Desiree
14 Japanese title: suffix
16 Scotch cutter
17 Swift steed
18 XY
19 Tennis star Mandlikova
20 Bowlines?
23 Old Testament bk.
25 Benet interest

# PUZZLE 86

## ACROSS

1 Work with wood
7 Abundant
9 Mark Lindsay hit of 1969
10 Columnist Barrett
11 Austen offering
14 Writings of: suff.
15 Nightingale's note
16 Sticking point
18 Shrink from
19 Ridicule (with "of")
21 Ridicule
22 Monopoly structures

## DOWN

1 Sacred beetle
2 Gas layer around the sun
3 Indignant
4 Judy's daughter
5 Nanki-__ (*Mikado* role)
6 Air
8 Dr. Zorba, on *Ben Casey*
12 Reciprocal
13 Factors
17 Seagull creator
18 Influence
20 Stark who was involved with Prince Andrew

## ACROSS

1 All shook up
7 Texas/Mexico border river, to Mexicans
9 Snake killer
10 Dos Passos trilogy
11 List item
13 "Hey, wait a __!"
14 Bud

15 Father of Lies
18 State of confusion
19 Mythical king of a race of Scandinavian dwarfs
21 Win over by wiles
22 Stylus

## DOWN

1 Revive
2 Reed
3 Science fiction writer Hubbard
4 *Comme il faut*
5 All the people
6 Move along at a speed of

7 Blue-collar sitcom
8 Idle
9 Put out of place
12 Safecracker
16 Undercover?
17 Astronaut Armstrong
20 Size: abbr.
21 Enclosed by

## PUZZLE 88

### ACROSS

1 Letter line
6 "And what if ___?"
9 Wise and able governor
11 Lake Victoria is its main reservoir
12 Clothed by
13 It's plucked
14 Eighth mo., once
16 Scottish "go"
17 Marlo's mate
19 *The Plug-In Drug* subject
20 One who minds what you eat
23 Dissonance
24 Well contents
25 Touch, for example

### DOWN

1 Compass dir.
2 Addis Ababa native
3 Sellout victim's recompense
4 Communications conglomerate: abbr.
5 Instinctive ability
6 Form of flattery?
7 Roy Rogers' partner
8 Only companion?
10 Bug-in-a-ruggish
15 Josip Broz, familiarly
18 Two smackers?
20 601, in Roman numerals
21 Colleague of Fidel
22 Comedian Louis

# PUZZLE 89

## ACROSS

1 Blend of sounds in a recording
4 Middlemost
8 "The Knight of the Cart"
10 Pindar product
11 Star star
13 Capital of Benin
15 Get ready to testify
16 Electric guitar pioneer Fender
17 It's been cured
19 Quits office
20 Cobb and Hardin

## DOWN

1 Grasslands
2 Sense-of-balance center
3 "The Mayor of Simpleton" rock group
4 Cobblestone clatter
5 Places for rest and recreation
6 Computer scientist Turing
7 Study of words and wordplay
9 Alcohol-selling establishments
12 Corners
14 Recounted thing
18 Peach center

# PUZZLE 90

## ACROSS

1 Not exceeding
7 Acceptable
9 Musical round that involves retrograde motion
11 Corleone's creator
12 Miami twins?
13 Swatch competitor
14 Syllable for Santa
16 D, in C
17 Shaq's pack
20 Map abbrs.
23 Comparable in certain respects
25 Number of people in a certain category
26 Printer's space
27 More than matches

## DOWN

1 Cartoon company
2 British streetcar
3 UFO, at times
4 __-Wan Kenobi
5 Renfrew resident
6 Hoglike creature of Malaysia
7 Seep
8 Fort __ (Kentucky military reservation)
10 Very many
15 Houston player
17 Horse hair
18 Prolific auth.
19 Caesar's partner
21 Sci-fi classic *Dune*
22 Transatlantic planes: abbr.
24 ". . . but for the grace of God __"

# P U Z Z L E   9 1

## ACROSS

1 Movie-maker, initially
4 Combination part
7 Dropping-sticks-in-water game inventor
9 First name in country
10 He gave Madonna choreography advice
12 Shy
13 Bugs Bunny co-creator
14 *The Thousand and One Nights* character
16 Just able to bear someone
18 Ages
19 Parting syllables
20 Faint
21 Put the kibosh on

## DOWN

1 EPA stat
2 Turns
3 Villechaize costar
4 Reagan treat
5 Baker predecessor
6 Reddish-brown
8 Bad guys, rolewise
9 Draw in
11 Biochemical cycle
14 Epileptic's warning
15 One opposed
16 Service site
17 Strain

## ACROSS

1 BMI competitor
6 Maxilla
9 Rosalind's cousin
10 __-Ida (Tater Tots inventor)
11 Bald man's bluff
13 Had in mind
14 *Head of the Class* actress
16 Bounders
17 White beast, in Algonquian
19 Wear for a sweater
22 Mama's boy
23 Exaggerated
24 Man. neighbor
25 Exclamation of disgust

## DOWN

1 Exclamation in Aachen
2 Large amount
3 Business that rips you off
4 Without wind
5 1962's "__-oom-mow-mow"
6 1965 Rookie of the Year
7 Followed the rainbow
8 Mourning clothes
12 Nightmare
14 "Why?"
15 Shopworn garment?
18 Check
20 Blue Eagle agcy.
21 Kind of condensation

# PUZZLE 93

## ACROSS

1 Lip
5 Blowout
9 Still-life subject
10 Resound
11 Stingy
13 Summer music
14 Line worker
15 New beginning
16 "I don't get it"
18 Function
19 Violation spotter
21 Gandhi's dad
23 Ambisinister
25 Couple
26 City north of Hamburg
27 Creating concupiscence
28 Preeminent member of a group

## DOWN

1 Corium coverer
2 Sketch out
3 Units of acceleration
4 Conductor Leinsdorf
5 Spell-off
6 .405 hectares
7 Hilton's paradise
8 Keep secrets from
12 Determined partner
17 Salome's stepfather
20 Bend
22 Water carrier
24 Name that's loved?

# PUZZLE 94

## ACROSS

1 Vase, at times
10 Mancini music
11 Peach mutation
12 Got to
13 Nettle
14 Mississippi feeder
16 Caprine comment
19 *The Sound of Music* villains
23 Supper, of sorts
25 Wacky platter spinner
26 Mom or apple pie, e.g.

## DOWN

1 Hawk home
2 Peasant, in Dutch
3 Support provider
4 Record
5 Lincoln, for one
6 DOS command
7 Half a city?
8 Odo player
9 "Bang a Gong" group
15 Bearded
16 Garden spots
17 Lee of song
18 Aussie rockers
20 Its number is 30
21 Analogy piece
22 Put away
24 Second word of a Fleming title

197

# PUZZLE 95

## ACROSS
1 Spout out
4 Start of an Andrew Sisters title
7 It's done for fun
11 Melbourne group of the '80s
12 Anna's author
13 Film part
16 Carroll creature
20 Son of Mnesarchus
22 Fall
23 Word that literally means "dung twig"
24 Pope's purview

## DOWN
1 Fix
2 Daughter of Marie and Pierre
3 907.18 kilograms
4 Life, for short
5 Pooh's friend's signature
6 Publicity
8 It was discovered by Galileo
9 Suffix used to indicate the salt of an acid
10 One with a cutie on the QT
13 Makes a bore bigger
14 Ragtime musical
15 Use a rubber
17 Start of a Gentry title
18 Word that literally means "love potion"
19 First name in cosmetics
21 Money regarded with contempt

# ANSWERS

## PUZZLE 1

## PUZZLE 2

```
PUZZLE 1
I B M ■ ■ G N A W
M E O W ■ R I T A
O L G A ■ A P E X
K L U T Z Y ■ ■
■ A L C O H O L
■ ■ H O A G I E
P U Z O ■ I R O N
E S A U ■ R E N D
W E P T ■ ■ S S E

PUZZLE 2
A D M I T ■ J U G
P R O N E ■ A G E
B U T T E ■ I L L
■ G H A S T L Y
■ S E C ■ W H A
■ T A T T O O S
J O T ■ O F U S E
I R E ■ R E S I N
M E N ■ T R E N D
```

## PUZZLE 3

## PUZZLE 4

```
PUZZLE 3
T K O ■ ■ G M A N
A N N ■ C A I R O
P O T H O L D E R
■ W H E W ■ D A M
■ ■ E X P E L
C D B ■ A B E T
H E A R T B E A T
A L L A H ■ A P E
P A L M ■ ■ R E D

PUZZLE 4
S E A T ■ ■ J I G
K A R A T ■ A N O
Y U C C A ■ C F O
■ C H I P ■ K I D
■ L E T I T B E
F A N ■ O R E L
L I E ■ C Y N D I
A R M ■ A S N E R
K E Y ■ ■ T Y R E
```

**PUZZLE 5**

| J | U | N | E | ■ | C | H | A | P |
|---|---|---|---|---|---|---|---|---|
| A | S | O | F | ■ | O | U | C | H |
| B | E | E | F | ■ | H | E | R | O |
| ■ | ■ | L | I | V | E | D | I | N |
| S | F | ■ | C | A | R | ■ | D | E |
| M | A | R | I | N | E | R | ■ | ■ |
| O | B | O | E | ■ | N | A | I | F |
| C | L | A | N | ■ | C | U | L | L |
| K | E | N | T | ■ | E | L | L | Y |

**PUZZLE 6**

| F | E | Z | ■ | ■ | ■ | F | I | X |
|---|---|---|---|---|---|---|---|---|
| U | R | I | S | ■ | A | L | L | Y |
| R | E | N | T | ■ | Q | U | I | Z |
| ■ | I | C | E | C | U | B | E | ■ |
| ■ | ■ | ■ | P | E | A | ■ | ■ | ■ |
| ■ | J | E | H | O | V | A | H | ■ |
| J | A | D | E | ■ | ■ | I | D | O | L |
| A | K | I | N | ■ | T | A | P | E |
| Y | E | T | ■ | ■ | ■ | M | I | X |

**PUZZLE 7**

| E | L | F | ■ | R | A | P | I | D |
|---|---|---|---|---|---|---|---|---|
| T | R | U | ■ | E | X | U | D | E |
| T | O | Z | ■ | D | E | F | E | R |
| U | N | Z | I | P | ■ | F | A | N |
| ■ | ■ | Q | E | D | ■ | ■ | ■ | ■ |
| E | T | C | ■ | P | O | L | K | A |
| G | R | U | M | P | ■ | Y | I | N |
| G | I | J | O | E | ■ | E | N | D |
| S | P | O | O | R | ■ | S | K | Y |

**PUZZLE 8**

| ■ | ■ | C | O | P | ■ | ■ |
|---|---|---|---|---|---|---|
| ■ | ■ | A | L | A | ■ | ■ |
| ■ | ■ | R | D | S | ■ | ■ |
| D | U | S | T | S | T | O | R | M |
| E | S | K | I | M | O | D | O | G |
| M | A | I | L | O | R | D | E | R |
| ■ | A | K | A | ■ | ■ |
| ■ | G | E | L | ■ | ■ |
| ■ | E | Y | E | ■ | ■ |

## PUZZLE 9

| E | M | M | A | | H | A | Z | Y |
|---|---|---|---|---|---|---|---|---|
| C | O | A | X | | O | H | I | O |
| H | O | S | E | | T | O | N | K |
| O | R | C | | J | O | Y | C | E |
| | | U | C | A | N | T | | |
| B | Y | L | A | W | | H | U | B |
| L | A | I | R | | Z | E | R | O |
| A | N | N | E | | A | R | G | O |
| S | K | E | W | | P | E | E | K |

## PUZZLE 10

| J | A | M | | P | A | N | D | A |
|---|---|---|---|---|---|---|---|---|
| A | L | A | | A | L | B | U | M |
| F | I | R | S | T | L | A | D | Y |
| F | A | I | T | H | S | | | |
| E | S | A | U | | T | E | E | M |
| | | C | I | A | R | D | I | |
| J | A | C | K | F | R | O | S | T |
| A | L | O | O | F | | D | E | E |
| B | E | N | N | Y | | E | L | S |

## PUZZLE 11

| E | B | B | S | | J | O | G |
|---|---|---|---|---|---|---|---|
| L | A | R | A | | L | O | B | O |
| F | L | A | N | | O | V | E | R |
| | L | E | T | S | L | I | D | E |
| U | P | | A | I | L | | I | N |
| N | O | T | A | R | I | Z | E | |
| Z | I | O | N | | P | E | N | H |
| I | N | G | A | | O | N | C | E |
| P | T | A | | | P | O | E | M |

## PUZZLE 12

| T | A | B | B | Y | | J | A | M |
|---|---|---|---|---|---|---|---|---|
| O | P | E | R | A | | A | M | Y |
| P | E | R | O | N | | Y | E | W |
| | | Y | O | K | O | | N | A |
| P | O | L | K | | L | A | D | Y |
| A | M | | S | W | I | M | | |
| Y | A | P | | E | V | I | T | A |
| T | H | E | | L | I | T | E | R |
| V | A | T | | K | A | Y | A | K |

202

## PUZZLE 13

```
J O S H ■ C O L A
I N T O ■ A P E X
M E R R I M E N T
■ ■ I N F E R N O
I R K ■ ■ ■ A Y N
S H E G O A T ■ ■
S I O U X C I T Y
U N I T ■ H O W E
E E L S ■ E N O S
```

## PUZZLE 14

```
T O B A C C O
S H A L L O W
A G R E E O N
R O B ■ O K
■ D I S P E L S
■ ■ H A ■ O H I
■ B A T H T U B
■ E N R O U T E
■ D E A D S E T
```

## PUZZLE 15

```
J A M ■ B U F F
A L A N ■ O V A L
G E R E ■ W A V E
■ S P A S ■ O X
■ W H O P P E R
H A ■ T E R N
O N E I ■ I D L E
O D E S ■ T E A L
P A L M ■ D I M
```

## PUZZLE 16

```
M R B I G ■ Z E E
P O R N O F I L M
H E A P ■ L O S S
■ G U Y A N A
■ ■ B E T
■ B E L A I R
C A N I ■ R U F F
P S Y C H O I I I
U S A ■ A N N E X
```

## PUZZLE 17

| A | L | F | I | E |   | J | A | G |
| W | E | A | N | S |   | I | V | E |
| L | E | T | T | E | R | M | A | N |
|   | M | A | E |   | A | B | L | E |
| N | A | S | A |   | T | O | A | T |
| A | J | A | R |   | H | U | N |   |
| H | O | P | S | C | O | T | C | H |
| U | R | I |   | A | L | O | H | A |
| M | S | G |   | B | E | N | E | T |

## PUZZLE 18

|   |   | W | H | O | M | P | S |
|   | T | R | A | L | A | L | A |
|   | M | A | I | N | D | R | A | G |
| T | E | X | T |   | J | U | G |
| A | S | A |   | O | D | E |
| S | S | T |   | G | R | I | D |
| S | A | I | L | B | O | A | T |
| E | G | O | T | I | S | M |
| L | E | N | G | T | H |   |

## PUZZLE 19

| J | I | B | E |   | J | E | E | P |
| A | V | E | R |   | A | M | M | O |
| P | E | T | S |   | M | E | M | O |
| E | Y | E |   | M | E | R | Y | L |
|   |   | N | O | I | S | Y |   |
| B | R | O | N | X |   | F | E | W |
| L | A | I | T |   | J | I | V | E |
| E | Z | R | A |   | A | L | I | A |
| W | E | E | P |   | W | E | L | K |

## PUZZLE 20

| O | F | F |   | I | C | I |
| P | E | E | L |   | M | A | N | I |
| C | R | E | A | M | P | U | F | F |
| I | D |   | M | O | R | S | E |
| T | I | M | E | P | I | E | C | E |
|   | N | I | N | E | S |   | T | V |
| C | A | L | E | D | O | N | I | A |
| O | N | E | S |   | N | E | O | N |
|   | D | R | S |   | E | N | S |

204

## PUZZLE 21

| S | P | C | A |   |   |   |
| E | R | I | C | I | D | L | E |
| M | O | N | T | R | E | A | L |
| I | F |   |   | E | A | V | E |
| S | O | M | E | P | L | A | C | E |
|   | R | O | T | E |   | T | V |
|   | M | A | T | A | H | A | R | I |
|   | A | N | A | T | O | M | I | C |
|   |   |   | P | A | C | T |

## PUZZLE 22

| A | C | M | E | S |   |   |
| C | H | E | R | U | B |
| L | A | M | A | R | R |
| U | F | O |   | F | I | X |
|   | F | I | L | B | E | R | T |
|   |   | R | I | O |   | A | H | A |
|   |   | Z | A | F | T | I | G |
|   |   | A | R | L | E | N | E |
|   |   | D | O | D | G | E |

## PUZZLE 23

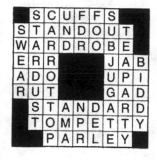

| | S | C | U | F | F | S |
| S | T | A | N | D | O | U | T |
| W | A | R | D | R | O | B | E |
| E | R | R |   |   | J | A | B |
| A | D | O |   |   | U | P | I |
| R | U | T |   |   | G | A | D |
| | S | T | A | N | D | A | R | D |
| | T | O | M | P | E | T | T | Y |
| | | P | A | R | L | E | Y |

## PUZZLE 24

| | C | H | O | C | T | A | W |
| T | O | O | T | H | A | C | H | E |
| A | L |   | B | E | N |   | I | Q |
| D | O |   | C | D |   | M | U |
| P | R |   | S | K | Y |   | S | I |
| O | F |   | A | M |   | I | N |
| L | A |   | G | A | P |   | C | O |
| E | S | T | A | T | E | T | A | X |
| | T | Y | L | E | N | O | L |

## PUZZLE 25

```
  A C C E D E S
  P R O R A T A
  P O T E N C Y
J A W       E Y M
O L D M A S T E R
B L O O D T E S T
    U D D E R
    T A L I A
    L E G
```

## PUZZLE 26

```
A R M A N I
M A R C O N I
Y M A   T U L I P
    N A I R O B I
L O D Z   E V E N
E N M A S S E
E A R L Y   Y A P
    S E N I O R S
    A C Q U I T
```

## PUZZLE 27

```
    L O B E
C H I L I D O G
H E A D L I N E
A L B   K E E N E
O I L       T U X
S P E E D   H I P
  A T R O P I N E
  D O G G E R E L
    S E N D
```

## PUZZLE 28

```
M A O       M I X
A S P S   T O R Y
C H E E Z W H I Z
  E C L A I R S
      L I N
  P O O R B O Y
C O F F E E P O T
A S I F   D U K E
P E T     S E X
```

206

## PUZZLE 29

| | W | A | S | H | T | U | B | |
| H | A | R | P | E | R | L | E | E |
| E | T | T | U | | I | N | A | N |
| R | E | E | D | | M | A | U | D |
| S | R | | | | | | G | O |
| E | M | I | T | | A | V | E | R |
| L | A | S | H | | L | E | S | S |
| F | R | E | E | S | T | A | T | E |
| | K | E | Y | H | O | L | E | |

## PUZZLE 30

| A | V | E | | | F | U | J | I |
| M | I | X | | C | E | S | A | R |
| I | C | E | | L | L | A | M | A |
| S | E | R | G | E | I | | I | Q |
| | S | T | R | A | N | G | E | |
| H | Q | | O | N | E | O | F | F |
| A | U | T | O | S | | B | A | A |
| N | A | I | V | E | | A | R | K |
| D | D | A | Y | | | D | R | E |

## PUZZLE 31

| S | S | S | | L | A | M | P |
| T | H | E | J | O | K | E | R |
| R | A | P | A | C | I | T | Y |
| E | N | T | W | I | N | E | |
| W | E | E | | | R | B | H |
| | | M | I | S | S | M | A | Y |
| | A | B | N | E | G | A | T | E |
| | R | E | L | A | T | I | O | N |
| | C | R | A | M | | D | N | A |

## PUZZLE 32

| A | Y | R | E | S | | |
| M | O | O | L | A | H | |
| B | O | O | K | L | E | T |
| U | H | F | | | X | R | A | Y |
| S | O | T | | | A | G | O |
| H | O | O | K | | | N | A | H |
| | | P | I | C | A | S | S | O |
| | | | D | O | V | I | S | H |
| | | | P | A | T | I | O |

**207**

## PUZZLE 33

```
Z I N C █ P E P A
I D E A █ A P E X
P A W N █ P O P E
█ █ A J A X █ █
█ I V O R Y █ █
█ M E G A █ █ █
A J A R █ Z O O M
G A G A █ Z U L U
A B E L █ I T E M
```

## PUZZLE 34

```
█ █ █ E V I C T
L A B R A D O R █
A L L A L O N E █
T A U █ █ J A G
E N D █ █ U S A
R A G █ █ R U M
█ L E E S H O R E
█ D O G E A R E D
█ A N G E L █ █
```

## PUZZLE 35

```
█ █ M I X █ █
█ M E R Y L █
Y O D E L E R
E P I S O D E
A H A █ P G A
T E E T H E D
S A V I O R S
█ D A R N S █
█ L E E █ █
```

## PUZZLE 36

```
█ P S A L M █
B R U S H U P
B E █ E P A █ O K
R A Z Z █ S P R Y
A L E C █ A U T O
S E E A █ A B E T
S R █ N A P █ N O
█ T H A T S I T
█ A L O O F █
```

## PUZZLE 37

```
J A P E _ W A K E
E V I L _ A S I A
D E C K _ V A N S
I R K _ J E R K Y
_ _ C L A R E _
J E L L Y _ S E W
O L E O _ M U S E
S L A Y _ S L A B
H A N D _ S T U B
```

## PUZZLE 38

```
A B B Y _ A B E L
P Y R E _ B O R E
P R E P _ Z O O M
O E R _ R U N T O
I Q _ K E G _ I N
N U K E D _ M C D
T E E N _ P A I R
E S P Y _ A L S O
E T T A _ W I M P
```

## PUZZLE 39

```
F A D _ W I F E
F L O _ I N O N
F I L M _ N E X T
_ C A V E R _
_ E X E R T _
_ V I X E N _
W H I M _ D E A F
T U T U _ S U B
S H A M _ S K I
```

## PUZZLE 40

```
O N A _ D O S E
F I J I _ R H E A
F L A N _ J A W S
_ C Z E R N Y
_ A L I K E _
C A N O P Y _
A V I V _ L O A F
S I T E _ L O C O
T S A R _ H E X
```

209

## PUZZLE 41

## PUZZLE 42

## PUZZLE 43

## PUZZLE 44

## PUZZLE 45

| B | A | C | H |   | C | R | A | G |
| A | L | O | U |   | O | O | N | A |
| S | E | L | F | I | M | A | G | E |
|   | R | E | F | F | E | D |   |   |
|   | T | R | I |   | O | H | A |   |
|   |   | I | N | A | F | O | G |   |
| I | N | D | E | X | F | U | N | D |
| K | E | G | S |   |   | I | S | E | E |
| E | W | E | S |   | T | E | S | S |

## PUZZLE 46

|   |   |   | J | A | B |   |   |   |
|   | T | R | I | P | O | D | S |   |
|   | S | E | V | E | N | U | P |   |
| J | A | M | E | S | D | E | A | N |
| O | R | O |   |   |   | D | R | Y |
| G | I | V | E | C | H | A | S | E |
|   | N | A | R | R | A | T | E |   |
|   | A | L | L | O | V | E | R |   |
|   |   |   | E | W | E |   |   |   |

## PUZZLE 47

| A | S | A | J | O | K | E |   |
| B | E | L | A | R | U | S |   |
| B | U | L | W | A | R | K |   |
| E | R | O | S |   | T | I | L | E |
| S | A | W |   |   | M | I | X |
| S | T | A | N |   | B | O | S | H |
|   | N | O | T | U | P | T | O |
|   | C | A | R | R | I | E | R |
|   | E | M | I | N | E | N | T |

## PUZZLE 48

| A | W | L |   | E | S | S |   |
| Y | O | U | N | G | L | A | D | Y |
| E | R | G | O |   | O | K | R | A |
|   | M | E | N | S | W | E | A | R |
| S | H |   | S | I | D |   | I | N |
| H | O | M | E | T | O | W | N |
| O | L | A | N |   | W | R | A | Y |
| P | E | R | S | O | N | A | G | E |
|   | V | E | X |   | P | E | W |

211

## PUZZLE 49

```
E P I T O M E
V E T O P O W E R
A R T Y   P E L E
G O O E Y   S E P
A X   D A B   G O
B I D   M Y L A R
O D I N   L E N T
R E S O N A N C E
  C H O W D E R
```

## PUZZLE 50

```
K I D   P A S S E
I D O   A L O H A
N E D   S I N E S
D O G I T   O L E
  L E F T O F F
L O B   E X A L T
A G A I N   G I O
M U L L S   U F O
B E L L E   N E L
```

## PUZZLE 51

```
A B C   W I L D
E R U D I T I O N
C A B I N E T R Y
  Z A P   M I M E
T E L     G I T
U N I T   B I T
R O B I N H O O D
F U R N I T U R E
  T E E N   S Y N
```

## PUZZLE 52

```
C O O P T
O N W A R D
B E L L Y A C H E
  L E A F L E T
A S I F   F O R E
M I K A D O S
P R E C E D E N T
    E D I T O R
    E L O P E
```

212

## PUZZLE 53

| P | R | A | M |   |   | J | I | G |
| A | U | R | A |   | F | U | N | T |
| P | E | T | S |   | I | N | S | O |
|   |   | C | H | A | R | G | E |   |
|   | F | A | N | B | E | L | T |   |
|   | A | R | O | U | S | E |   |   |
| P | I | N | T |   | A | G | E | S |
| A | T | E | E |   | L | Y | L | E |
| S | H | Y |   |   | E | M | M | A |

## PUZZLE 54

| M | O | T | I | O | N | S |   |   |
|   | E | R | I | T | R | E | A |   |
|   | D | I | S | D | A | I | N |   |
| J | I | G |   |   |   | G | T | D |
| A | C | I | D |   | C | H | A | R |
| M | A | N | I | L | A | B | A | Y |
|   | T | A | K | E | N | O | N |   |
|   | E | L | E | C | T | R | A |   |
|   |   | S | H | O |   |   |   |   |

## PUZZLE 55

| M | E | S | A |   | B | L | A | B |
| S | A | H | L |   | R | I | P | E |
| G | R | O | K |   | I | G | E | T |
|   |   | R | A | J | A | H |   |   |
|   | A | T | L | A | N | T | A |   |
|   | S | H | I | M | M | E | R |   |
| J | O | A | N |   | A | N | O | N |
| A | N | N | E |   | Y | U | M | A |
| B | E | D |   |   | P | A | P |   |

## PUZZLE 56

|   |   |   | F | R | E | S | C | O |
|   |   | B | O | E | R | W | A | R |
|   | P | A | G | A | N | I | N | I |
| T | U | B |   |   |   | Z | O | O |
| I | R | A |   |   |   | Z | E | N |
| B | I | L | L | F | O | L | D |   |
| I | S | O | L | A | T | E |   |   |
| A | T | O | D | D | S |   |   |   |

213

## PUZZLE 57

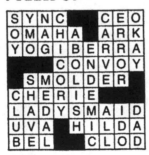

```
A B B R     Z A P
C L I E N T E L E
E A S T E R E G G
  H O R S E
    N O M A S
      F I T C H
A M B I T I O U S
L O A T H S O M E
F O G     E P E E
```

## PUZZLE 58

```
    N E A P
  H E A V I E R
W A N T E D T O
A R G O N A U T
X V I     L A P
  A N T E D A T E
  R E A S O N E R
  D E C A N T S
    R O U T
```

## PUZZLE 59

```
S Y N C     C E O
O M A H A   A R K
Y O G I B E R R A
      C O N V O Y
  S M O L D E R
C H E R I E
L A D Y S M A I D
U V A   H I L D A
B E L     C L O D
```

## PUZZLE 60

```
  G R A T I S
  C O T T O N T O
  O L E A N D E R
P H D     S E E S
R E F     C P O
U R I S     E I N
D E N I Z E N S
E N C R O A C H
  T H E O R Y
```

## PUZZLE 61

```
. D A D . R I B .
. O L E . E G O .
S O O T . C O A T
T R U E N O R T H
U P . R R R . H A
B R I G A D O O N
S I D E . H O U K
. Z E N . O Z S .
. E A T . P E E .
```

## PUZZLE 62

```
B O A R S . D A D
O R S O N . I C E
P A S T A . E R E
. L A U G H T E R
. I N . U P . .
M A L D E M E R .
A R A . G A P E S
Z E N . A N S E L
E A T . D E I F Y
```

## PUZZLE 63

```
A T S E A . B Y A
F O N D D U L A C
A G O . O P A R T
R A W E R . C D S
. W H A C K . .
M P H . T B O N E
A L I B I . P O D
R A T I O N A L E
E Y E . N O L A N
```

## PUZZLE 64

```
A C C . . C O P
S A R A . S A G E
S P U N . K I D D
. E X A M I N E R
T V . G A P . N O
W E A R D O W N .
E R M A . L E A F
A D A M . E A S E
K E N . . K H Z
```

## PUZZLE 65

```
S P C A
P R A M
A I R B I L L
  M A R Q U E E
  E C O   C O G
  D A S H I N G
    S E A L A N E
        L R O N
        E D G E
```

## PUZZLE 66

```
S P R I G   C C V
H A I K U   A H A
A N D E S   P E N
H A     H O R S E
  M R F I X I T
G A H A N     D A
O H O   E B S E N
B A D   S O R E N
I T A   S W I P E
```

## PUZZLE 67

```
A B A   B A S T E
M A C   E T H A N
F I R     K I N D
M O O D R I N G
    P R O N G
  Z O O T S U I T
N O L O     A S H
F L I P S   R E A
L A S S O   D E W
```

## PUZZLE 68

```
S O H O   O C H S
K H A N   S H O E
I N R E   C R U X
P O D   H A I R
    T I E R S
  J I N X   T I N
P U M A   J I V E
E D E N   A N E W
P O S E   M A S T
```

**216**

**PUZZLE 69**

```
O P A L   P B A
R E C O V E R Y
S A U C E P A N
O C T   X Y Z
N E A T   S I K H
  B O G   L O Y
  C O L D S N A P
  O V E R R U L E
  B E T   S T A R
```

**PUZZLE 70**

```
    B L A M E
  H A L I F A X
  E P I S T L E
Z A P   P E D R O
I D L E   R I C H
P R I D E   V I M
  E Q U A T E S
  S U C R O S E
  T E E N Y
```

**PUZZLE 71**

```
J E H     W A X
A V A     A R M
K E L P   T I G E
E N L I G H T E N
  M I N O R I N
D O N K N O T T S
A N D Y   B O I L
T E E     U N O
A Y N     T A P
```

**PUZZLE 72**

```
  C A S C A D E
  B O S P O R U S
E A T   A S C O T
T I T A N I C
C L O G   N O V A
  N E M E S I S
M A G O O   I L K
T A I L B O N E
V A N D Y K E
```

## PUZZLE 77

```
T I M E B O M B
E G O M A N I A
R O O T L E S S
M T N   L I B
S A S     E M S
  H I T   H A T
  S I N E W A V E
  O N C E O V E R
  S E A N P E N N
```

## PUZZLE 78

```
      M A M A S
    S P E L U N K
    A R A L S E A
    L O L I T A
  F O X   N A R
  U N I S O N
P R I M I N G
L O C A T E S
O R A L S
```

## PUZZLE 79

```
A A F A I R
P R O M N I G H T
S C O T   D I E U
O A T H S   V E X
  D R E I D E L
P I E   D R U B S
T A S K   A P O P
A N T O N I O N I
    S O N N E T
```

## PUZZLE 80

```
  D R I F T S
  R O B B I E
J A S M I N E
O W E   A D S
B O W     P E W
  N A T   E A R
    T A R B A B Y
    E M P I R E
    R A M B L E
```

## PUZZLE 81

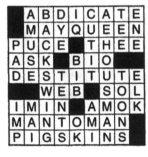

```
D O R I S D A Y
S K I N T O N E
T E N S E ■ D M C
■ ■ T U M ■ Y E R
P R I M ■ D R N O
E O N ■ S E E ■
P A T ■ C A N D O
■ M I N O R K E Y
■ S N O W Y O W L
```

## PUZZLE 82

```
M I A S M A ■
E D W O O D J R
R Y E B R E A D
■ ■ ■ R A Y S
■ ■ O I L ■
O F F S ■ ■
D E A D H E A T
D E G A U L L E
■ E Y E L I D
```

## PUZZLE 83

```
■ A B D I C A T E
■ M A Y Q U E E N
P U C E ■ T H E E
A S K ■ B I O ■
D E S T I T U T E
■ W E B ■ S O L
I M I N ■ A M O K
M A N T O M A N
P I G S K I N S ■
```

## PUZZLE 84

```
■ C H A O S ■
S L A C K O F F
H A L T ■ L I L I
A R F ■ L O M
M A I ■ T O P
I B N ■ R D A
R O C K ■ W A L L
■ W H I T E T I E
■ T I B E T
```

## PUZZLE 85

| B | A | M | B | I | ■ | J | U | G |
| B | R | I | E | F | C | A | S | E |
| S | A | M | E | ■ | O | V | E | N |
| ■ | P | E | R | S | U | A | D | E |
| ■ | ■ | H | A | S | ■ | ■ | ■ | ■ |
| S | A | M | A | N | T | H | A | ■ |
| O | R | A | L | ■ | E | A | R | N |
| D | A | L | L | I | A | N | C | E |
| A | B | E | ■ | Q | U | A | S | H |

## PUZZLE 86

| S | C | U | L | P | T | ■ | ■ | ■ |
| C | O | P | I | O | U | S | ■ | ■ |
| A | R | I | Z | O | N | A | ■ | ■ |
| R | O | N | A | ■ | E | M | M | A |
| A | N | A | ■ | ■ | J | U | G | ■ |
| B | A | R | B | ■ | H | A | T | E |
| ■ | M | A | K | E | F | U | N | ■ |
| ■ | S | C | O | F | F | A | T | ■ |
| ■ | H | O | T | E | L | S | ■ | ■ |

## PUZZLE 87

| ■ | ■ | J | O | L | T | E | D | ■ |
| ■ | R | I | O | B | R | A | V | O |
| M | O | N | G | O | O | S | E | ■ |
| U | S | A | ■ | E | N | T | R | Y |
| S | E | C | ■ | ■ | E | Y | E | ■ |
| S | A | T | A | N | ■ | F | O | G |
| ■ | N | I | B | E | L | U | N | G |
| I | N | V | E | I | G | L | E | ■ |
| N | E | E | D | L | E | ■ | ■ | ■ |

## PUZZLE 88

| S | E | R | I | F | ■ | I | D | O |
| S | T | A | T | E | S | M | A | N |
| W | H | I | T | E | N | I | L | E |
| ■ | I | N | ■ | L | U | T | E | ■ |
| ■ | O | C | T | ■ | G | A | E | ■ |
| ■ | P | H | I | L | ■ | T | V | ■ |
| D | I | E | T | I | C | I | A | N |
| C | A | C | O | P | H | O | N | Y |
| I | N | K | ■ | S | E | N | S | E |

**221**

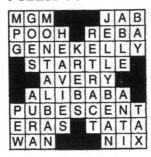

## PUZZLE 93

| E | D | G | E | ■ | B | A | S | H |
| P | E | A | R | ■ | E | C | H | O |
| I | L | L | I | B | E | R | A | L |
| D | I | S | C | O | ■ | E | N | D |
| E | N | ■ | H | U | H | ■ | G | O |
| R | E | F | ■ | N | E | H | R | U |
| M | A | L | A | D | R | O | I | T |
| I | T | E | M | ■ | O | S | L | O |
| S | E | X | Y | ■ | D | E | A | N |

## PUZZLE 94

| O | B | J | E | T | D | A | R | T |
| M | O | O | N | R | I | V | E | R |
| N | E | C | T | A | R | I | N | E |
| I | R | K | E | D | ■ | V | E | X |
| ■ | ■ | ■ | R | E | D | ■ | ■ | ■ |
| B | A | A | ■ | N | A | Z | I | S |
| E | U | C | H | A | R | I | S | T |
| D | R | D | E | M | E | N | T | O |
| S | A | C | R | E | D | C | O | W |

## PUZZLE 95

| J | E | T | ■ | ■ | B | E | I |
| A | V | O | C | A | T | I | O | N |
| M | E | N | A | T | W | O | R | K |
| ■ | ■ | L | E | O | ■ | ■ | |
| R | E | E | L | ■ | T | O | V | E |
| E | U | R | I | P | I | D | E | S |
| A | B | A | S | E | M | E | N | T |
| M | I | S | T | L | E | T | O | E |
| S | E | E | O | F | R | O | M | E |

**223**